teenVirtue

REAL ISSUES, REAL LIFE...A TEEN GIRL'S SURVIVAL GUIDE

teenvirtue

REAL ISSUES, REAL LIFE...A TEEN GIRL'S SURVIVAL GUIDE

by vicki courtney

B&H
PUBLISHING GROUP

Nashville, Tennessee

Teen Virtue: Real Issues, Real Life…
A Teen Girl's Survival Guide

Published by B&H Publishing Group, Nashville, Tennessee

ISBN: 978-0-8054-3056-1

Dewey Decimal Classification: 248.83
Subject Heading: YOUTH—RELIGIOUS LIFE/CHRISTIAN LIFE

7 8 9 10 11 12   11 10 09

virtuousreality.com

AUTHOR WEB SITES TO CHECK OUT

www.virtuousreality.com—features online magazine for preteen, teen, college, and adult women.

www.virtuousreality.com/events—provides a schedule of upcoming Yada Yada and Yada Yada Junior events for girls ages third through twelfth grades and mothers; also information about how you can bring an event to your area.

www.vickicourtney.com—to view Vicki Courtney's current speaking schedule or to find information about inviting her to speak.

www.virtuepledge.com—features an online community where girls and young women can pledge themselves to biblical virtue.

OTHER BOOKS BY VICKI COURTNEY FROM BROADMAN & HOLMAN

Your Girl: Raising a Godly Daughter in an Ungodly World

Yada Yada: A Devotional Journal for Moms

More Than Just Talk: A Journal for Girls

The Virtuous Woman: Shattering the Superwoman Myth

Table of Contents

INTRODUCTION

Being a girl in today's culture is hard. Everywhere you turn, messages are telling you to be thin, pretty, sexy, assertive, self-confident, and do what ever it takes to make guys drool.

Don't you wish the teen years came with an instruction manual? I would have given anything to have had a guidebook to help me navigate through difficult issues like low selfworth, breakups, annoying siblings, and the real biggie: not making the cheerleading squad.

Little did I know I had an instruction manual all along! Unfortunately, it sat on a shelf in my closet and gathered dust. My grand-parents had given me a children's Bible for Christmas when I was ten years old; and while I knew the Bible was a special book, I had no clue it was my instruction manual for life. I didn't go to church, so I wasn't sure how or where it fit into my life. Even so, I was drawn to it during times when I was sad, confused, or in the middle of some sort of crisis. I would take it off the shelf, crawl up on my bed, and flip through the crisp pages searching for something, anything to calm my anxious heart. If only I had had some sort of survival guide to help me decipher the code.

TeenVirtue was written to be that survival guide. It addresses common issues girls your age face and points you to just the right passages in the Bible. Believe it or not, God cares about girl politics, boy problems, breakups, embarrassing moms, roller-coaster emotions, broken hearts, and much more. He never intended for you to go at it alone in the world. The layout is similar to that of a magazine and contains short, easy-to-read articles and quizzes. But unlike the average fashion magazine geared to girls your age, this guide emphasizes *virtue* over *vogue*. The word virtue is certainly not a common word you hear among teens of today. Think about it. How many times have you heard someone say, "Do you know so-and-so? She is so virtuous!" Yeah, I thought so. *Virtue* is defined as "moral excellence, strength, and purity." Not topics you hear much about in the fashion magazines! In fact, most of the fashion magazines seem to dwell more on how *not* to be virtuous.

Proverbs 31:10 says, *"Who can find a virtuous woman? for her price is far above rubies"* (KJV).

Take a look at an average sampling of teen girls, and you might be left asking the same question: "Where are the good girls?" I realize there is not much encouragement nowadays to be a *good girl*, but in the end those who pursue virtue will reap the rewards. The choice is yours: Do you want to be a rare find with worth far above rubies? For the price of a few mocha frappuccinos, *TeenVirtue* can help you reach your goal.

Kick back, relax, and enjoy. Also check out www.virtuous reality.com, an online magazine for girls your age. Join the virtue movement, spread the word, start a trend, and together let's make virtue a reality!

—Vicki Courtney

Beauty Inside Out

the *sexy* craze

'd be lying if I told you it wasn't nice to be noticed every once in a while.

t's everywhere you look. The word *sexy* is so overused. I'm not even sure we know what it means anymore. Next time you're at the supermarket, I dare you to try and find one fashion magazine without the word *sexy* on the cover. Sexy jeans. Sexy lips. Sexy swimsuits. Sexy handbags. Can a purse be sexy? Give me a break! So what's up with the sexy craze? And better yet, why do we care?

When I looked up the word *sexy* in the dictionary, I found two definitions. One says this: "arousing or tending to arouse sexual desire or interest." The other one says: (slang) "highly appealing or interesting; attractive."[1] I'm going to go out on a limb here and assume that in the majority of cases, the word is used as slang and the latter definition applies. Show me a single handbag that makes a guy want to have sex with you, and I might change my mind. I think you get my point.

So what's wrong then with Christian girls buying into the "be sexy" message? It boils down to a question of motives. For some girls, "sexy" is not about looking attractive or appealing, which the slang term implies; "sexy" is about arousing the opposite sex. Girls who seek to arouse guys are often labeled as a tease. The sad thing here is that many girls never stop and think about what happens if their "be-sexy-arousal-plan" works. Was the final goal to have sex with the intended target or just be noticed? Can they "tease" guys without the guys assuming they are willing to "please" them, as well? Girls, don't be fooled by the fashion magazines—you don't have to arouse guys to get them to notice you.

For many girls your age, the sincere motive is to look attractive, not so much sexy. I'd be lying if I told you it wasn't nice to be noticed every once in a while. If we're honest, we can all probably admit to wanting to turn a few heads. What girl doesn't remember the compliments they receive from guys? Especially if it comes from that cute guy you happen to like. Is it really a sin to look attractive? No, it's not. In fact, God would want you to take care of yourself. Remember, your body is the temple of the Holy Spirit, and we should take pride in his temple. It drives me crazy when Christians imply that women should seek to look plain and sometimes even frumpy when decorating his temple. I like to look attractive, and I'm not afraid to admit it.

Looking attractive is not a sin, but it does become a sin if your motive is to arouse the opposite sex. It becomes a sin if the end result would disgrace rather than compliment God's temple. It becomes a sin if you care more about what others will think rather than what God thinks. In the end, sexy just doesn't seem like a word that God would want others to use when describing the very residence in which his Spirit resides. ✱

---

1. *The American Heritage® Dictionary of the English Language, Fourth Edition* (New York: Houghton Mifflin Company, 2000).

By now you have probably been warned about the dangers of smoking. You have probably been warned about the dangers of drinking and drugs. You have probably been warned about the dangers of the Internet. But have you ever been warned about the dangers of flipping through fashion magazines? In a 1995 study, researchers found that 70 percent of the women who looked at fashion magazines reported feeling depressed, guilty, and ashamed of their bodies after only one to three minutes of viewing the pictures of the models scattered throughout the magazines.[1]

WARNING:
FASHION MAGAZINES CAN BE DANGEROUS TO YOUR HEALTH

What really gets me is that these same magazines will run damage-control articles that encourage women to accept their body shapes. Yet, if you flip through the average fashion magazine, you would be hard-pressed to find a model that represents the average American woman who is a size 14. Wait, I take that back. Many of them probably are a size 14—in the children's department. The magazines tell you one thing to get on your good side and make you think they care about the problem of body image, but the real proof is in the models they choose on their pages. I believe there is a word that describes that kind of behavior—hypocrisy.

But that's not the only way the teen fashion magazines demonstrate hypocrisy. They preach about "girl power" and encourage girls to be independent and strong, yet just about every issue is filled with advice about what it takes to get a guy to look in your direction. They tell you what to wear

> **70 percent of the women who looked at fashion magazines reported feeling depressed, guilty, and ashamed of their bodies after only one to three minutes of viewing.**

to make guys drool or what to do to keep a guy, and they send an overall message that you are a big nothing unless you have a guy on your arm. What is really ironic is that this message comes after the women's liberation movement of the 1970s. Sure girls are going to like guys, but wouldn't it be better if we attracted them with our minds and hearts rather than the magazines's snag-a-man tactics? Today's magazines portray girls and women as sex objects and send a message that we are here in this world to please and satisfy men. Some girl power, huh? I assure you, you are worth more than that.

And what about the encouragement in these magazines for girls to be sexually active? I could fill an entire book with blatant examples of ways the articles, pictures, advertisements, and advice columns imply that sex is nothing more than a recreational hobby. They make it seem like everyone is doing it and you're some kind of freak if you're still a virgin. Many of the editors of these magazines defend their content by saying this is what girls really want to hear. That's a cop-out. The bottom line is that they want to make money and in order to make money and sell magazines; they have to push the limit with their content. Don't be fooled—they are not looking out for you. In fact, they are using you to make money. They are laughing all the way to the bank while teen girls flip through their magazines and become more and more disillusioned and depressed.

Believe it or not, I used to subscribe to *Seventeen* and *CosmoGirl* a couple of years ago. The magazines provided fresh examples of the brainwashing messages to be thin, to be sexy, to be promiscuous, and to get a boyfriend. My purpose for subscribing to these magazines was to share the fresh examples at my conferences to teen girls and their mothers across the country. It gave me great pleasure to shed light on the magazine's hidden agenda. However, I no longer subscribe to the magazines because what I was finding became more than I could emotionally bear. After

The dictionary defines the word agenda as "a temporally organized plan."[2] Before you flip through an average teen fashion magazine, you need to know that the editorial team has thought long and hard about the content that should be contained on the pages. The editorial staff knows that the more they expose their readers to controversial topics and put a positive spin on them, the more likely their readers will come to accept certain immoral behaviors as normal. And this is exactly what is happening in our culture today. Many have lost sight of right and wrong, good and evil.

The editorial staff knows that the more they expose their readers to controversial topics and put a positive spin on them, the more likely their readers will come to accept certain immoral behaviors as normal

reading them each month, I found myself becoming depressed and heartbroken over what young women your age were being exposed to. I recall one issue that had an article dealing with incest. It went into graphic detail and acted as if the average girl would encounter incest in the course of her life. I recall another issue that did a "Love Stories" feature for the month of February in honor of Valentine's Day. One of the featured stories was about Jessica and Meghan, two lesbian teen girls who were in love. The feature included an excerpt describing how they met, their first kiss, and how blissfully happy they are today. The magazines even included a picture of them kissing each other on the mouth! But the one article that will forever stay etched in my mind was about a teen girl who had decided she really wanted to be a boy. The article described how she was saving her money to have a full sex-change operation. She had already had her breast tissue removed, and the article included a picture of her naked from the waist up. As if the picture wasn't enough to scar me for life, the content in the article was so graphic that I cannot in good conscience repeat it, lest it scar you as well. Girls, these magazines have an agenda to sway you into thinking all these things are normal.

Magazines like *Seventeen* were a big part of my teen years, and it saddens me to see how they have negatively changed over the years. Knowing what I know after flipping through them and others such as CosmoGirl, I cannot allow my own daughter to look at them for fear she will be damaged emotionally by what is on the inside. I know there are many who will read this and think I'm going way overboard, but

Advice columns imply that sex is nothing more than a recreational hobby.

remember the research. Why pay for a product that leaves a majority of girls feeling depressed in just three short minutes of using it? If you care at all about your emotional well-being, stay far away from fashion magazines. If you have already subscribed, consider canceling your subscription and using your back issues as liner for your gerbil cage. If you cancel, just do me a big favor—write the editor to let her know you wised up to their agenda. Oh, and tell her your gerbil says, "Thanks."

1. Study by Laurie Mintz, www.ABCNews.com, 30 October 2002.
2. *WordNet®* 2.0, © 2003 Princeton University.

making peace with your BODY

Have you ever stood in front of your mirror and grumbled, "I hate my body"? Have you ever wished you had longer legs, a flatter stomach, or bigger boobs? Do you wish you were fatter, thinner, taller, or shorter? Have you figured out by now that Barbie's shape is totally messed up? In fact, I read that if Barbie's measurements were projected to life-size, her measurements would be 38-18-34 (a figure not found in nature.) Even if you were one of the few girls who weren't allowed to play with Barbie, chances are you are just as warped as the rest of us when it comes to body image issues.

Do you remember playing for hours with your "Happy to Be Me" doll? Probably not. It came out in the early 90s and was marketed as an alternative to Barbie. It claimed to have more realistic body proportions than Barbie and was marketed to parents as "A Doll That Both You and Your Child Will Love." Sorry to take a little bunny trail here, but isn't it interesting how they chose to use the word *child* instead of *daughter*. Talk about being politically correct. Did they really think little boys were saving up their allowance to buy a "Happy to Be Me" doll? That's more warped than Barbie's figure. I would love to write a letter to the company and politely explain that the world is a better place when little boys play with GI Joes, not "Happy to Be Me" dolls. Unfortunately, I can only dream about writing that letter because the company is no longer in business. The dolls were a flop, and the company went kaput, proving that in the end most girls prefer to play with a doll that has an unrealistic body shape—a shape we can never have.

Besides, it's not fair to blame just Barbie for the negative attitudes among women concerning body shape. Honestly, I played with Barbie, and I can't remember ever thinking, *Wow, I wish I had her bod.*

Even if you are currently overweight or underweight, you can still aspire to reach a healthy weight range and at the same time accept yourself.

I do remember thinking, *Wow, I wish I had her Corvette.* For the record I didn't get her bod or her car.

As someone who struggled off and on with an eating disorder, I can attest to the power of the message to be thin coming from media, magazines, and the culture. I wanted desperately to look in the mirror and like the image staring back at me. Unfortunately, this would not come until I hit my thirties and I finally came to the conclusion that life is too short to dwell on something as superficial as having a perfect body. After almost two decades of having a love/hate relationship with my body, finally, with God's help,

"I praise you because I am fearfully and wonderfully made; your works are wonderful, I know that full well."
(Psalm 139:14 NIV)

I made friends with my shape. I decided that my contentment would no longer be based on the readout on the scale or how I looked in a swimsuit. I was going to like me, no matter what.

Now, don't get me wrong, I'm not recommending that we just let ourselves go, eat five boxes of Twinkies, and blow off exercising. I'm talking about accepting our shape for what it is, whether it's pear shaped, apple shaped, hourglass, short, tall, big boned, or petite. Even if you are currently overweight or underweight, you can still aspire to reach a healthy weight range and at the same time accept yourself.

The true test is to be able to look at ourselves in a full length mirror and confidently say to God, "I praise you because I am fearfully and wonderfully made; your works are wonderful, I know that full well" (Psalm 139:14 NIV).

If you can't say it and mean it, consider posting the above verse on your mirror as a reminder and say it every day. Pray and ask God to help you believe it. ✳

?DID YOU KNOW?

- If shop mannequins were real women, they would be too thin to menstruate and bear children.

- **There are three billion women on the planet who don't look like supermodels and only eight who do.**

- Marilyn Monroe, Hollywood sex goddess, wore a size 12.

- **If Barbie were a real woman, she'd have to walk on all fours. Because of her unrealistic proportions, she could not balance on her long legs and tiptoes.**

- The average American woman weighs 144 pounds and wears a size 12 or 14.

- **One out of every four college-aged women use unhealthy methods of weight control, including fasting, skipping meals, excessive exercise, laxative abuse, and self-induced vomiting.**

- Models in fashion magazines are airbrushed and retouched. In real life they look more like the rest of us than their glossy print images.

- **Twenty years ago models weighed 8 percent less than the average woman. Today they weigh 23 percent less, and many fall into an anorexic weight range.** ✳

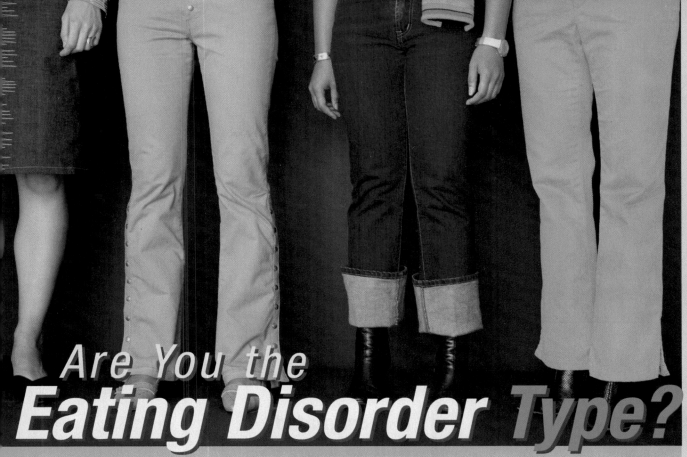

Are You the Eating Disorder Type?

On a recent trip to the local Starbucks, the gal in front of me ordered a low-fat-grande-vanilla-no-foam-two-sweet-n-lows-decaf-latte. In the time it took her to say it, I could have balanced my checkbook. Clearly this gal was on a diet. I recognized the familiar diet language from my own past experience of trying to shave every calorie off a grande latte yet still have something left in the cup in the end. Ah, the fond memories of a chronic dieter. As I stepped up to the counter, I felt a twinge of guilt as I ordered a vanilla latte with all the extras. Give me the foam, the sugar, the whole milk. Was I experiencing a weak moment of abandoned willpower? Not exactly. My past history of chronic dieting was not a result of struggling with a weight problem but quite the opposite. You see, I used to have an eating disorder. Fortunately, my disorder never required hospitalization, but a few times my weight plunged as low as 100 pounds on my five-foot, five-inch frame. I now consider myself recovered, but I still wrestle from time to time with the temptation to "control" my weight by limiting necessary calories.

During my college years my love/hate relationship with food began. During my freshman year I gained the traditional "freshman 10" plus a few extra pounds to boot. Prior to college, I had always been the athletic type and on the thin side. Weight had never been a problem for me until college. **Dorm food, fast food, and food at all hours of the day and night without exercise began to take its toll on me.** For four years of college, my weight would fluctuate up and down by as much as thirty pounds. At one point I was just a few pounds shy of my weight plunging into the double digits. I was subsisting on saltines, fruit, and diet sodas and obsessed with working out, sometimes, twice a day. My wake-up call came when I passed out at the health club during a workout. Any resolve I made to "get better" was short-lived, and before long food was once again my enemy. This attitude consumed my thinking each and every day of my college years. If my weight went over 110 pounds, I felt guilty, miserable, and disgusted with myself.

least one area of your life—your weight. My three most serious bouts with anorexia came at times when I perceived circumstances in my life were out of my control.

For others, it will serve as a way to get attention. Unfortunately many people will unknowingly contribute to this disorder when paying compliments to those with borderline eating disorders. I was amazed at the amount of favorable praise I received from girls in high school and college when I had an eating disorder. I looked liked nothing more than a frail skeleton, and girls would say, "You look great!" My all-time favorite was, "What is your secret to staying so thin?" Amazingly, the comments that most infuriated me came from only a handful of friends. They had the boldness to be honest about the situation and said things like, "You look terrible," or, "Are you OK? I'm worried about you." Ironically their negative form of attention motivated me in my quest to get better.

3. It is a spiritual issue. When someone is deep in the throws of an eating disorder, building a relationship with Jesus Christ is rarely at the top of their priority list. They are consumed with food—not Christ. In John 5:6, Jesus asked a crippled man by the pool of Bethesda before he healed him, "Do you want to get well?" It seems strange that Jesus would ask this of someone who had been lame for thirty-eight years, yet it is a critical question in a healing process.

If you have an eating disorder, can you take the first step by answering the question Jesus posed to the lame man? Do you want to get well? If your answer is a confident "Yes," then share with someone you trust that you need help. My first step in the healing process came when I was finally able to acknowledge, "I want to get well." Acknowledging that you have a problem is only the first step, and it may be necessary to see a Christian counselor or someone in the medical field if your condition is serious. If you are ready, help is on the way. The Great Physician is in . . . will you see him?[2] *

It is estimated that as many as one-third of high school girls show some symptoms of an eating disorder. Even if you don't have an eating disorder, chances are, you know someone who does. I am not a professional counselor, but I want to offer you some basic truths that helped me in my own recovery.

With an eating disorder three basic issues are at the core of the problem:

1. It is a physical issue. The body responds to starvation by slowing certain bodily processes. Other possible effects are a decrease in blood pressure, slowed breathing, and a cease in menstration. Skin can become dry, and hair and nails become brittle. Reduced fat causes the body temperature to fall. As body chemicals become imbalanced, heart failure can occur.[1]

2. It is an emotional issue. I remember when my parents would become concerned and tell me, "Just eat!" Though their motives were pure, it is similar to telling an alcoholic, "Just stop drinking!" When attempting to help someone with an eating disorder, it is rarely enough just to hammer at them with pleas to eat or give them facts about the damage they are doing to their body. Beneath the surface of every eating disorder is a feeling of low self-worth and disgust in regard to body image. For some it will stem from a control issue—when other things in life are in disarray and out of control, there is a sense of comfort in being able to control at

> ## It is estimated that as many as **one-third** of high school girls show some symptoms of an eating disorder.

1. Dixie Farley, "On the Teen Scene: Eating Disorders Required Medical Attention" (www.fda.gov/fdac/reprints/eatdis.html).
2. According to a presentation at the 2001 annual meeting of The Society for Adolescent Medicine. Over 5000 students from 152 high schools nationwide were surveyed about their eating habits (www.drgreene.com/21_343.html and www.drgreene.com/21_343.html).

dressed to *Lure* or be *Pure?*

My boys are obsessed with fishing in a pond set back in a wooded area behind our house. Because this pond can only be accessed by a few homes in our neighborhood, it is well stocked with fish of every kind. My boys never get tired of hiking back there with their nets, poles, and tackle boxes. They shimmy carefully out onto a homemade makeshift dock perched atop a leaning tree and cast their lines into the water. Their quest: Catching one of the big-mouth bass who will occasionally swim teasingly near the surface of the water. Trust me, these fish are not big by accident. These guys have had the run of the pond for years—that is, until my boys came along. Fortunately, my boys are only interested in the challenge of catching them, and once they do, they pull out the hook and throw them right back in for a second chance. (That's your cue to say, "Ahhhhhhh, poor little fishies.") Both my

Many girls are unaware that the clothes they wear can act as bait.

boys insist that snagging these big 10 to 12 pound bass come down to the bait. They rely on fancy spinner lures that attract the curious fish with shimmering pieces of metal and rubber tentacles that dangle from a hook.

So, what in the world does fishing have to do with the way girls dress? Given the scanty fashions of the day, many girls are unaware that the clothes they wear can act as bait—the kind that attract boys. You've probably noticed by now that girls and guys are wired differently. When it comes to attraction, girls tend to be more emotionally wired while guys tend to be more visually wired. An article appeared in my local paper titled "What Girls Wear, and What Boys Think" that proves this point. A sampling of boys we're interviewed at the local mall and asked what they thought of some of the girls who walked by wearing hip-hugger jeans with bare midriffs and scanty tops. One boy suggested that girls dress that way because they want attention. Another boy said it is an "invitation." He said, "They're telling you, 'Come get it.' When girls dress like that, it tells guys they're easy."[1]

The truth hurts. **For many girls, their sincere motive in wearing skin-baring fashions is to be fashionable. Unfortunately, there is no denying that guys read much more into it than a sincere fashion statement.** Just like the lures my sons use to attract the fish they catch, your clothes may be sending out an invitation to the guys that you never intended to send. Some girls are fully aware of the power they can have over the opposite sex when it comes to cultivating their sensualities with just the right outfit, whether it's a cleavage-baring top, short shorts, a bare midriff, or tight-fitting clothes. For them, negative attention is better than no attention at all. Regardless of whether or not a girl's motives are to be fashionable or to be sensual, the results are the same. Like the bass drawn to just the right bait, guys will be drawn to you but for all the wrong reasons. When the fish see bait, they see a free meal, and they get it to go. Do you want to send that kind of message to the guys?

The Bible actually addresses how women should dress. First Timothy 2:9 says, "I also want women to dress modestly, with decency and propriety" (NIV). The actual word for "propriety" is a Greek word, *sophrosune*, which means "sanity or soundness of mind."[2] Let me translate the verse for you: Do the clothes you wear indicate that you've lost your mind? I am shocked at how many Christian girls who should know

> Dressing modestly not only demands respect from the guys but is a sign of self-respect.

better show up at church (or anywhere else, for that matter) dressed inappropriately. I recall a Sunday morning service where one of the girls in the youth group took part in a skit. She was wearing a skirt that was small enough to fit my five pound Yorkie. Clearly she hadn't thought this through, and when she went to sit down during the skit, her skirt was eye level of the audience, and she ended up flashing everyone in the congregation, including the pastor on the front row! Now c'mon. There's nothing cool about that!

Here's the bottom line when it comes to modesty: **You want what you wear on the outside to allow others to focus on God rather than you.** I am certainly not saying you have to dress like a nun. It is possible to dress both fashionably and modestly but it will take some effort and extra time spent looking for clothes that would pass the test. Take God shopping with you next time and when you look in the mirror, ask him what he thinks. His opinion is the only one that matters. Remember, if you are a Christian, your body is

the temple of his Holy Spirit, so he has a vested interest in how you choose to adorn his temple. You also want to be certain that what you wear reflects who you are on the inside. That way, when a guy is drawn to you, it will be for the right reasons.

Dressing modestly not only demands respect from the guys, but it is a sign of self-respect. It makes the statement that you feel good enough about yourself without having to dress in such a way that would "lure" the wrong kind of attention. Get in the habit of doing a mirror check before you head out the door and ask yourself, Is this outfit screaming "lure" or "pure"? ✱

1. "What Girls Wear, and What Boys Think" *Austin American Statesman*, April 2001.
2. *Strong's Greek & Hebrew Dictionary*, © 1993. Used by permission on Online Bible, Winerbourne, ONT. All rights reserved.

I WANT TO GET MY BELLY BUTTON PIERCED

Q: All my friends are getting their belly buttons pierced, but my parents won't let me do it. I don't understand what the big deal is— I mean, they let me get my ears pierced. What's the difference?

A: There is not a Bible verse that says, "Thou shalt not pierce thy belly button," but here are some important factors to consider:

What is the purpose? First Timothy 2:9 tells women to dress modestly, so technically girls should not be wearing clothes that expose their midriffs. If you are living by God's Word, why pierce something that you are going to cover up all the time? Most girls who pierce their belly buttons do so with the intent of showing it off—not covering it up.

Consider the actual effect it has on guys. Some Christian girls try to justify piercing their belly buttons by saying they intend to cover it up except for when they are wearing a swimsuit. Piercing your belly button is different from piercing your ears. While I understand that many girls innocently want to pierce their belly buttons because it is the current fashion trend, believe me, it will send a different message to the guys. There is no arguing that a pierced belly button is considered by most to be sensual and even sexual. Case in point: If you put two girls side by side who are wearing the same swimsuit, and one has a pierced belly button and the other one does not, and then line up a group of guys and ask them which girl was more likely to have loose morals, the majority of the guys would pick the girl with the pierced belly button. In the end, do you want to risk sending a signal to guys that you may be willing to compromise sexually? I hope not.

Think about the future. One sample group of students who opted to have their belly buttons pierced indicated that it took approximately thirty-eight weeks for it to heal verses the standard six weeks for pierced ears.[1] Again, that's a heavy sacrifice for a Christian girl who plans to cover it up. For those who are willing to assume the risks and attempt to justify it with the claim that it can always be removed, it is not uncommon for a navel piercing to tear or leave a permanent scar.

Many girls fail to think past the moment and evaluate what a pierced belly button would look like ten, twenty, thirty-plus years later. You will spend the majority of your years in adulthood, and the truth is, most adult women are not running around flashing their midriffs to show off their pierced belly buttons. Try to picture yourself ten to twenty years from now at the neighborhood pool party with your kids. Better yet, try to imagine your mom with a pierced belly button. OK, you get my point, right?

What would God say? First Corinthians 6:19–20 says this: "Do you not know that your body is a sanctuary of the Holy Spirit who is in you, whom you have from God? You are not your own, for you were bought at a price; therefore glorify God in your body."

This is a hard concept to understand, but the truth is, if you are a Christian, your body doesn't belong to you—it belongs to God. In the end you must ask yourself, Would piercing my belly button bring honor to God? Just as we discussed with the issue of immodest fashions, God wouldn't want you to decorate his temple with something that has sexual undertones. Life is full of situations where your desires and God's will won't always line up, and you will be faced with choosing your way or God's way. The temporary and fleeting satisfaction of piercing your belly button could never match the long-term and lasting satisfaction of submitting to his good, pleasing, and perfect will (see Romans 12:2).

---

1. See www.schoolnurse.com/med_info/body_piercing.html.

to
Tattoo
or not to
Tattoo

I love to people watch, so I was in heaven as I sat under my beach umbrella while on vacation with my family at a popular Florida beach destination. I consider myself more in touch with youth culture than most people my age, so I should not have been surprised at the number of girls with tattoos who paraded up and down the beach. At one point my teenage son was with me, and I asked him what he thought about the tattooing trend among girls. He said that he didn't care for it but that most people his age didn't think it was a big deal. However, he held strong opinions about older women who were tattooed.

It doesn't make sense to tattoo God's temple without his permission.

"Older" in his book was anything in the upper twenties. His exact words were, "That's just sick. . . . What were they thinking?" When I pointed out that someday the younger girls would be in the "older" category, his face grimaced. I'm not sure he had ever made the connection that what appeared to be "no big deal" among the girls his age, would be labeled "sick" in the near future.

Tattooing is very popular, and chances are good that you know someone who has gotten one. I realize that this is something that has become more culturally acceptable among the younger generation, but there are some important factors to consider before a Christian girl marks her body in a permanent fashion.

First, girls need to consider the feelings and wishes of their parents. If your mom and dad are adamantly opposed to tattoos, you have an obligation to respect their wishes while living under their roof and on their dime. Chances are good that they are opposed based on one or more of the following reasons listed below. The truth is, they probably have their own story of making a split-second decision in their younger years that seemed right at the time but instead, yielded lifelong consequences. They are looking out for your best interests.

Second, many Christians are opposed to tattooing because the Bible specifically says, "You are not to make gashes on your bodies for the dead or put tattoo marks on yourselves; I am the LORD" (Leviticus 19:28). While it is true that the order not to mark our bodies is considered under the old covenant that was replaced with the death of Christ and the law of grace, this does not mean that we ignore the principles behind many of the laws of the Old Testament. Similar to the issue of body piercing, we need to remember that a Christian's body is considered a temple or dwelling place of the Holy Spirit. It doesn't make sense to tattoo God's temple without his permission. I am willing to bet that few Christians actually seek out God's will when they are weighing the decision to get a tattoo. Does this mean that God would say no to every Christian who sincerely seeks his will in regard to tattooing? Not necessarily. While I am personally opposed to tattooing, it is not for me to say it is wrong in every case. God may say yes to someone who sincerely views it as an expression of their love for Christ and an opportunity for it to serve as an outward expression of their faith. Again, call it a hunch, but I seriously

Tattoo

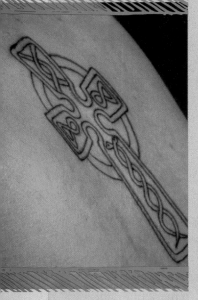

doubt that the majority of tattooed Christians have processed their decision in such a spiritually mature fashion.

Third, girls should consider the long-term effects of having a tattoo. Having a tattoo removed is costly and painful, so one should think past the moment and consider whether or not this permanent marking will be something they desire in the years to come. Regardless of whether or not it is acceptable to the younger generation, many surveys indicate that most people consider tattoos to be a sign of rebellion and low class. When it comes to finding a job, 42 percent of managers said they would have a lowered opinion of someone who is tattooed (or pierced). Even worse, 58 percent said they'd be less likely to offer a job to a tattooed (or pierced) applicant![1] Again, I think of the older women that I witnessed on the beach who had tattoos, and I wonder how many of them made the decision to tattoo on a spontaneous whim in their younger years. What seemed cool then, now looked ridiculous. (Ditto for navel piercing.)

Another reason that girls should think past the moment when deciding whether or not to tattoo is the ever-changing fashion trends. Tattoos at one time were fashionable among those in the grunge era. When the Britney fashion era followed, with its signature midriff, cleavage-baring blouses, and microminis, tattoos seemed to cross over as a fashion statement among the average suburban teen. However, as I write this, a new fashion trend is emerging among teen girls. The skin-baring fashions seem to have taken a backseat to knit polo shirts with emblems, ruffled skirts with ribbons, and a look that is altogether conservative, preppy, and clean-cut. If only I had saved my Izod shirts from my own high school years! There is no denying that tattoos and preppy don't mix. Fashions change over the years, and trends will come and go. Even if the preppy fashion trend is short-lived, it is only a matter of time before tattoos will be considered outdated.

Last of all, I couldn't help but stereotype the girls (and guys) on the beach who had tattoos. **The girls who were free of tattoos and piercings seemed more innocent and confident.** The mere fact that they had not given in to the trend spoke volumes about their character. Again, I have no argument with those who have taken the matter before God and view their tattoo as a symbol of their faith and a means to witness to others, but for the vast majority this is not the case. If you are among the tattooed who are reading this and did not seek God's counsel when making your decision, do not feel shame. Consider it a valuable life lesson and move on. That's what the message of grace is all about. ✱

1. Hans H. Chen, "Tattoo Survey Results: Vault Explains It All for You" (www.vault.com/nr/main_article_detail.jsp?article.jsp?article_id=5319842&ht_type=5).

extreme
makeover

my daughter was one of those beautiful babies that got attention everywhere she went. She was extremely small for her age and had beautiful fair skin, blonde curly hair, blue eyes, and a sparkling personality. When she started walking, people often commented that she looked like a walking porcelain china doll. Everywhere we went, she attracted oohs and aahs. In the beginning I loved the attention she got and would just smile proudly when people would comment.

I remember one time when she was about three years old and she said something to indicate that she was more than aware of the attention she had gotten for her looks. We were walking along a sidewalk and she caught a glimpse of her reflection in a shop window and said, "Oooh, pwiddy gull." At the time I thought it was perfectly adorable and indicated a high self-esteem. Unfortunately I was still buying into the world's worth equation: worth = what you look like. So by default I pushed the same faulty equation off on my daughter.

However, about a year later when she was in preschool, I realized we had a problem. It was picture day at her school, and she put on her prettiest dress with the matching hair ribbon. When I dropped her off at the door that morning, her teacher said, "Paige, you are such a pretty girl." And instead of saying, "Thank you," my child brushed by her teacher with a sideways glance and said, "I know. Everyone tells me

world of hurt when she hit the gawky preteen years. Fortunately, today, as a teen, she is not the least bit haughty or proud. She does not build her worth in or on anything as hollow as fading beauty.

My heart is grieved over shows like *Extreme Makeover* and *The Swan* that send a message to girls in the viewing audience that self-esteem is all about the outside package. I cringe when I hear the contestants talk about how their "self-worth" is defined after having surgical procedures. What happens when the natural aging process kicks into effect and things start to fall apart? What happens if they gain weight? What happens if people stop noticing they are attractive? I guess their worth will plummet again. I would love it if they did a follow-up story in fifteen to twenty years. Would the "swans" still be flying high? Would the *Extreme Makeover* contestants be drained of their esteem and their money from keeping up with the necessary tune-ups along the way?

that." I was mortified! After that, I quit making comments about her external beauty and tried to downplay it when others made comments. Besides, everyone knows that cute kids don't always grow up to be cute adults. If I had continued to allow her to define her worth by her outward appearance, I would be setting her up for a

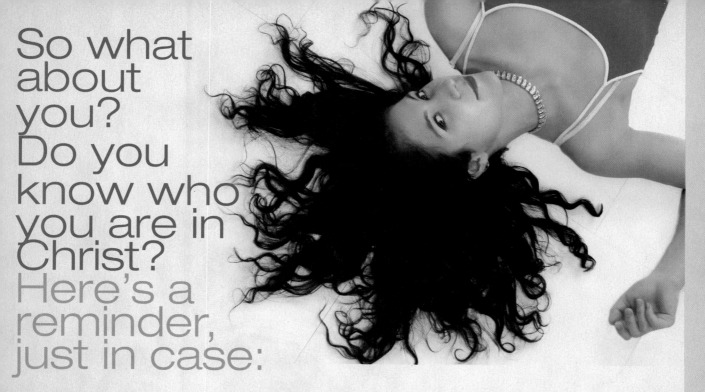

So what about you? Do you know who you are in Christ? Here's a reminder, just in case:

You are the light of the world. A city situated on a hill cannot be hidden. (Matthew 5:14)

But to all who did receive Him, He gave them the right to be children of God, to those who believe in His name. (John 1:12)

I have called you friends, because I have made known to you everything I have heard from My Father. (John 15:15)

And if children, also heirs—heirs of God and co-heirs with Christ—seeing that we suffer with Him so that we may also be glorified with Him. (Romans 8:17)

You did not choose Me, but I chose you. I appointed you that you should go out and produce fruit and that your fruit should remain, so that whatever you ask the Father in My name, He will give you. (John 15:16)

Don't you know that you are God's sanctuary and that the Spirit of God lives in you? (1 Corinthians 3:16)

Therefore if anyone is in Christ, there is a new creation; old things have passed away, and look, new things have come. (2 Corinthians 5:17)

He made the One who did not know sin t
be sin for us, so that we might become the righ
eousness of God in Him. (2 Corinthians 5:2

I have been crucified with Christ; and I no longer live, but
Christ lives in me. The life I now live in the flesh,
I live by faith in the Son of God, who loved me and gave
Himself for me. (Galatians 2:19–20)

For you are all sons of God through faith in Christ Jesus. For
many of you as have been baptized into Christ have put
Christ. (Galatians 3:26–2

Because you are sons, God has sent the Spirit of His Son into
our hearts, crying, "Abba, Father!" So you are no longer a
slave, but a son; and if a son, then an heir through God.
(Galatians 4:6–7)

For He chose us in Him, before the foundation of the world,
be holy and blameless in His sight. In love He predestined us
be adopted through Jesus Christ for Himself, according to H
favor and will. (Ephesians 1:4–

In Him we have redemption through His blood, the forgiveness of our trespasses, according to the riches of His grace. (Ephesians 1:7)

For we are His creation—created in Christ Jesus for good works, which God prepared ahead of time so that we should walk in them. (Ephesians 2:10)

And you have been filled by Him, who is the head over every ruler and authority. (Colossians 2:10)

So if you have been raised with the Messiah, seek what is above, where the Messiah is, seated at the right hand of God. (Colossians 3:1)

Therefore, God's chosen ones, holy and loved, put on heartfelt compassion, kindness, humility, gentleness, and patience. (Colossians 3:12)

For you are all sons of the light and sons of the day. We're not of the night or of darkness. (1 Thessalonians 5:5)

But you are a chosen race, a royal priesthood, a holy nation, a people for His possession, so that you may proclaim the praises of the One who called you out of darkness into His mavelous light. (1 Peter 2:9)

Look at how great a love the Father has given us, that we should be called God's children. And we are! The reason the world does not know us is that it didn't know Him. (1 John 3:1)

He saved us—not by works of righteousness that we had done, but according to His mercy, through the washing of regeneration and renewal by the Holy Spirit. This [Spirit] He poured out on us abundantly through Jesus Christ our Savior, so that having been justified by His grace, we may become heirs with the hope of eternal life. (Titus 3:5–7)

SO, HOW ABOUT YOU? Have you had an extreme makeover of the heart? The next time you have an identity crisis, refer back to this list as a reminder of who you really are. This beats being "pwiddy" any day. ✱

NOT YOUR Grandma's WORLD!

*E*ver wonder what it was like when your grandma was a teenager?

We know that teenagers growing up in the 1940s through the 1960s didn't have cable, computers, and cell phones. We do know that there were some things in common like boys, school, and parents. Other than that, it was a much different world. If they couldn't instant message (IM), text message, watch cable, or rent their favorite DVD, what in the world did they do to fill their days?

Would you believe that they did have fashion magazines? In fact, *Seventeen* was actually launched in 1944. It is amazing to compare the articles, ads, and pictures from the early issues of that magazine to the current versions of the same teen magazine. Flipping through some of the old magazines gives us a glimpse of what life was like for the average teenage girl growing up in the late 1940s to the early 1960s.

Did you know that issues of *Seventeen* magazine from 1945 to 1960 included an average of ten ads for sterling silver flatware, diamond engagement rings, and china? It was clear that marriage and family were on the mind of the average teenage girl in Grandma's day.

What about today? Well, you can forget about the pro-marriage ads. In fact, I couldn't find any hint or mention of marriage as a future option in today's magazines.

What about the relationships between teenage girls and guys in the 1940s to 1960s? Again the images in ads and articles hint at what it was like in Grandma's day. Notice the obvious respect the guys have for the girls in the pictures below.

In this 1950 *Seventeen* magazine cover the young man is reading her poetry. Yeah, like that happens a lot today!

The teen fashion magazines of today are full of images of guys and girls with their hands all over each other. In fact, most pictures show the girls as the aggressors or the ones in charge. Each magazine contains countless images of girls sitting on guys' laps or straddling them and sporting facial expressions loaded with attitude.

What about the topics of interest for the average teen girl in Grandma's day? Many articles dealt with art, music, friendship, faith, and family. In the articles that addressed parents, there was always encouragement to obey and respect your parents, whereas many articles in the teen magazines today treat parents as if they are clueless idiots who are out to sabotage their daughters' lives. As for common topics of interest in today's magazines, Grandma would be shocked to find articles on oral sex, homosexuality, incest, birth control, and cross-dressing teens. Wow, we've sure come a long way.

Unlike issues of today's magazines, the issues of teen magazines from Grandma's day did not have subtitles like "22 Jeans that Scream 'Nice Butt,'" "Swimsuit Tops that Tease and Please," and "How to Be a Guy Magnet." So, if Grandma didn't have advice on how to be a guy magnet or what to wear to make guys drool, how in the world did she ever manage to snag Grandpa? Surely she didn't attract him with her mind or heart—that just wouldn't be right, would it?

Teenage girls in Grandma's day may not have had e-mail, a buddy list, or an I-POD, but they generally had respect from guys, faith, and a love for family. At first glance, it may seem like they were missing out on a lot, but if you ask me, when it comes to the important things in life, maybe we're the ones missing out. ★

FEAR FACTOR

> Charm is deceptive, and beauty is fleeting; but a woman who fears the LORD will be praised. (Proverbs 31:30)

A truly beautiful woman is a woman who fears the Lord. This is not the same kind of fear that means to "be afraid." **To fear the Lord is to be in awe of him, to revere him, to respect him.**

And check out the benefits that come to those who fear the Lord:

1 Hallelujah! Happy is the man who fears the LORD, taking great delight in His commandments. (Psalm 112:1)

2 You who fear the LORD, trust in the LORD! He is their help and shield. (Psalm 115:11)

3 He will bless those who fear the LORD—small and great alike. (Psalm 115:13)

4 How happy is everyone who fears the LORD, who walks in His ways! (Psalm 128:1)

5 Then you will understand the fear of the LORD and discover the knowledge of God. (Proverbs 2:5)

6 To fear the LORD is to hate evil. I hate arrogant pride, evil conduct, and perverse speech. (Proverbs 8:13)

7 Whoever lives with integrity fears the LORD, but the one who is devious in his ways despises Him. (Proverbs 14:2)

8 In the fear of the LORD one has strong confidence and his children have a refuge. (Proverbs 14:26)

EMOTIONS:

CAN YOU TRUST THEM?

i have the absolute cutest dog on earth. She is so cute that cars stop and comment on her when I take her for a walk in my neighborhood. She is full grown and a whopping five pounds. She has the face of a bear cub, and her fur is as soft as chenille. One look and she would melt your heart.

> As your body goes through many changes, it will often affect your hormones and cause your moods to fluctuate.

When my family was in the market to buy a puppy a couple of years ago, I researched breed after breed in search of the perfect dog. I knew I wanted a small dog that, wouldn't shed, and had loads of personality. I chose the Yorkshire terrier breed because it seemed to match my preferences. I found a breeder and within months my little Lexie was born. She only weighed eleven ounces when we brought her home when she was six weeks old.

Now Lexie is full grown, and she has completely lived up to the description of her breed. She is small, she doesn't shed, and she has loads of personality. In fact she has loads of personalities.

I believe there is a medical term for this—Multiple Personality Disorder. She goes by a variety of names in our home: Psycho Pup, Devil Dog, and Lucy (short for Lucifer). One minute she can be the sweetest, most charming puppy on earth; and the next minute, she can turn into a snappy, feisty, growling pit Yorkie. In fact, I often joke that we didn't get a Yorkshire terrier—we got a Yorkshire terror.

There have been times when she has charged at my teenage son, growling and baring her teeth and sent him

girl talk

running in fear of his life. Mind you, my son is a macho athlete who is nearly six feet tall. Imagine what a sight it is when I find him standing on the sofa screaming for help at the top of his lungs while this five pound fur ball with an angelic face and pink hairbow sits at the base of the sofa baring her teeth just waiting for a piece of him. Within minutes she can completely reverse gears, wagging her tail and rolling over begging to have her stomach rubbed. She will then smother you with wet dog kisses, and you will wonder how you could have ever been afraid of something so sweet and harmless.

Talk about mood swings. While you may not be able to relate to mood swings that severe, I'm willing to bet you have experienced some sudden, fluctuating moods in your teen years. As your body goes through many changes, it will often affect your hormones and cause your moods to fluctuate. One minute you can be laughing, full of life, and social; and the next minute you can be in tears, worn out, and wanting to be alone. Can you relate? If so, you need to know that this is normal, and it won't always be this way. While there is not a whole lot you can do about your fluctuating mood swings, you can learn to manage them. Here are some things to remember the next time you feel a mood swing coming on:

Avoid making sudden spontaneous decisions during this time. When you are emotional, you can easily blow things out of proportion and overreact.

One minute you can be laughing, full of life, and social; and the next minute you can be in tears, worn out, and wanting to be alone.

Have at least one person that you can talk to. Make sure this person understands what you are going through and will be empathetic and remind you that it is temporary. It is ideal if this person is your mother, but I realize that not *all* girls have the luxury of a close mother/daughter relationship. You need an older woman you can trust that understands what you are experiencing and is at the other end of it. Avoid leaning on someone your age when you experience mood swings, especially guys!

When you are moody, try writing your thoughts down in a journal. This beats pouring your heart out to everyone you know.

Lean on Christ. Make it a habit to pour out your heart to Christ when you are feeling low. The sooner you learn to lean on the source of all comfort, the better.

Whatever you do, don't medicate your pain with drugs, alcohol, overeating, undereating, secular music with harmful and depressing lyrics, promiscuity, or any of the other common outlets that many teens your age run to in times of distress. Run to Jesus and let him fill your heart with a settled peace.

The most important thing to remember is that the frequency of mood

Trust in the LORD with all your heart, and do not rely on your own understanding; think about Him in all your ways, and He will guide you on the right paths. (Proverbs 3:5–6)

swing in the adolescent years rarely carries over to your adult years. If your moods seem more severe and more frequent than those of your friends, you need to let your parents know. You could have a chemical imbalance that can cause depression. Fortunately there are many ways to treat depression. Most importantly, should you ever find yourself thinking about suicide as an option, immediately tell an adult that you trust. If one of your friends even so much as hints at suicide (even jokingly), tell an adult that you can trust. Your friend may be mad at you initially, but it could end up saving his or her life.

Emotions can be managed and suicide is never an option.

If you are like most girls, the frequency of your mood swings should die down as you complete puberty, and your menstrual cycle becomes more consistent. Some girls will continue to experience PMS (premenstrual syndrome) at some level over the years, and this is completely normal. Hopefully your mood swings won't be as vicious as my Lexie's and send everyone running in fear!

Trust in the LORD with all your heart, and do not rely on your own understanding; think about Him in all your ways, and He will guide you on the right paths. (Proverbs 3:5–6) ✱

THINGS TO REMEMBER
the next time you feel a mood swing coming on:

1

Lean on Christ!

2
Don't make sudden or spontaneous decisions.

3
Have at least one person that you can talk to.

4
Avoid leaning on someone your age when you experience mood swings, especially guys!

5 try writing your thoughts down in a journal.

6
Don't medicate your pain with drugs, alcohol, overeating, under eating, secular music with harmful and depressing lyrics, or promiscuity.

7 Run to Jesus and let him fill your heart with a settled peace.

STAYING INLINE WHEN YOU'RE ONLINE...

I know it's hard for teens today to realize what life was like before the Internet. Back in the olden days, we had to go to the library to look things up. We had to call our friends on their home phones if we wanted to get in touch with them. If you were lucky, you had your own phone line. I remember the frustration of trying to reach a friend and hearing the busy signal. We didn't have call waiting, so I had to keep trying until the line was clear. Some of my friends were brave enough to do an "emergency breakthrough" where you call the operator and give her the number you are trying to reach. She asks your name and then breaks into the line and announces that there is an "emergency call" and gives your name. I was always too afraid to try it because I heard that sometimes the operator will stay on the line to see if it's really an emergency. Today, if you want to reach someone, you have many options. In fact, most teens don't even call the home line anymore. They just dial their friend's cell phone number. If they don't answer their phone, then you can send a text message, leave a voice mail, or log on to see if they are online. If they are online, they can zip them an IM and have immediate contact.

But I'm not so sure all this instant availability hasn't come with a price. With this freedom to communicate on the spot comes a freedom to say things that you might not otherwise say. I am one of those moms who knows how to spot-check my kid's buddy lists from time to time. I am amazed to read some of the profiles from "good kids" in the youth group. Many profiles include questionable lyrics pulled from secular songs, shout outs with suggestive comments, links to inappropriate sites, and comments from previous IMs that have been cut and pasted and often appear misleading when taken out of context. Technology in and of itself is not evil, but if we're not careful, it can definitely be a medium that Satan uses to sway many from the path of Christ. If you truly desire to stay "inline when you're online," consider following this code of conduct.

girl talk

TOP 10 ONLINE RULES

1 Try to get in the habit of asking yourself on a regular basis, "Would what I am typing bring glory and honor to God?"

2 If you have a profile, would someone who doesn't know you determine that you are a Christian after reading it?

3 Do people readily share gossip with you online? If so, don't feel flattered. They gossip with you because you have a proven reputation for participating in it.

4 Be cautious when clicking through to links provided on other people's profiles. Many are mislabeled and lead to inappropriate sites.

5 Always imagine that what you are about to type could be copied and pasted by the other person and used against you in the future. If what you are going to say is not something you are comfortable with others reading, don't type it.

6 Never talk bad about someone else . They could be sitting right next to the person you are IMing!

7 Hold other Christians accountable if they use bad language or have inappropriate comments or links on their profiles by gently challenging them to clean it up.

8 Make sure your screen name is edifying to God. I was shocked that one of my daughter's friends from camp had the screen name that partly read "Christianbabe." Her name alone sends a contradictory message.

9 Remember that e-mail and IM messages are often misunderstood because it's hard to read the emotion or intent behind the messages. Save your serious conversations for the phone or, better yet, face-to-face. And whatever you do, never, ever end a relationship by e-mail, IM, or text message!

10 Always remember that many parents have software installed on their home computers that can track every IM, every e-mail sent or received, every keystroke made, and every Web site visited. Whenever you e-mail, IM, or send a text message to someone, just assume for all practical purposes, that their parents will see it at some point! Most important, remember that God doesn't need a software program to track your keystrokes!

Last but not least, live by Philippians 4:8 which says, "Finally brothers, whatever is true, whatever is honorable, whatever is just, whatever is pure, whatever is lovely, whatever is commendable—if there is any moral excellence and if there is any praise—dwell on these things." ✱

do you have a Potty Mouth?

there's only one thing worse than a girl who cusses, and that's a Christian girl who cusses. You may wonder why we would even need to cover this, but trust me, this is an issue for many Christian girls. Many teens are exposed to bad language on a daily basis at their schools, and after hearing it day in and day out, it is easy to pick it up if you're not careful. This is not meant to excuse the behavior but rather to address it.

So, what about you? Do you find yourself slipping and using bad language? Maybe you have a potty mouth, and you don't even realize it. Sometimes we think "bad language" is only the real serious words used, and we justify other words that have become socially acceptable. Take this quiz to find out.

You just had your room completely made over by one of those home decorating reality shows. You walk in and say:

a) "Oh my God!"

b) "Oh, wow!"

c) "This is (BLEEP) great!"

Your friend just got her schedule, and she didn't get the same lunch as you. You are more likely to say:

a) "That sucks!"

b) "That stinks!"

c) (Something that would send your Grandma runnin' for a bar of soap)

You accidentally slam your locker on your finger. You are more likely to say:

a) "Crap!"

b) "Ouch!"

c) (Something that would make a mother cover her child's ears)

You just found out that this girl who drives you crazy at school now likes your boyfriend. You tell another friend:

a) "She is such a (bleep)."

b) "Join me in praying for my enemies."

c) Let's just say it's something that would make an old lady blush.

You are talking to your friend and you finish this sentence "I just got back from the mall, and I didn't get _____."

a) a friggin' thing.

b) a thing.

c) a (double BLEEP) thing.

If you have grown callous to hearing God's name misused, you need to worry.

If you answered anything other than (b), it's time to clean up your language. Our words are extremely important and reflect our true nature. Whether we like it or not, people will hold us to a higher standard if we say we are Christians. When we join in with the rest of the world by talking like the rest of the world, it is confusing to unbelievers who are watching or listening.

As a Christian, I was grieved in my heart when I hear anyone (Christian or not) use the Lord's name in vain, yet it is used all too freely in our culture. It is nearly impossible to sit through even a PG-13 movie and not hear the Lord's name taken in vain countless times. As Christians, we should take every opportunity to politely ask people to refrain if they use the Lord's name in vain. God's name should never be followed with an expletive and "Jesus Christ" was never meant to be a phrase uttered in frustration. The same thing goes for anything that would follow the word *holy*, including *cow*! I know this sounds ultra picky, but if you are not phased by blasphemy, then you need to go back and review the Ten Commandments. So important was this issue to God that he addressed it in the seventh commandment when he said, "Do not misuse the name of the LORD your God, because the LORD will punish anyone who misuses His name" (Exodus 20:7).

To this day I recall an incident in my college years at a football game. I was not a Christian, and my friend and I were talking in the stands before the game started. Unfortunately, my friend and I were using bad language and I must have used the Lord's name in vain. A lady sitting in front of us turned around and said something to the

effect of "Please, please, I have tried so hard to remain silent. Use any word you want, but I beg you not to use the Lord's name in vain." At the time we stared back at her like she was some kind of alien even though I did utter a polite apology to her. Her boldness did, however, cause me to think about it in the future and planted a seed that God deserves our reverence and respect.

Today I am like that woman in the stands at the football game. I cringe when I hear bad language, but I especially shudder when I hear the Lord's name used in vain. If you say it in my presence and I hear you, I will politely ask you to refrain. I have also encouraged my kids to have the boldness to do the same. While it would be impossible for them to call down every person using "bad language" at their schools, I have told them that there is absolutely nothing wrong with respectfully telling someone who blasphemes God's name, "You really shouldn't say that." If you have grown callous to hearing God's name misused, you need to worry.

Finally, make an effort to live by Ephesians 4:29 that says: "No rotten talk should come from your mouth, but only what is good for the building up of someone in need, in order to give grace to those who hear." ✶

You really shouldn't say that!

girl talk

CONFESSIONS FROM

Miss Popular

the immediate reward of countless invitations to spend the night, phone calls from boys, and ultimately, the ID bracelet of the most popular boy, which signified we were officially going steady. I remember reading and rereading the many comments in my yearbook after the signing party. My heart would swell with pride and worth every time one of my peers used words like *pretty* or *popular* or commented on how good I was at track and gymnastics. Once I experienced the approval of

Ahhhh, the joys of being popular. Cool friends, cool parties, cool clothes, cool life. I should know, as a past member of the esteemed popular group in middle school and high school. What girl in the world doesn't want more than one cute guy asking her to go to homecoming? Or her friends arguing about who gets to sit next to her at lunch? Or being at the top of the cool party list? While being popular definitely has its perks, don't be fooled into thinking it is an instant ticket to happily ever after.

I'll never forget the day I was voted most popular girl in the sixth grade. With the title came

others, I was hooked. In the months that followed, my life was consumed with maintaining the title of most popular girl. What if they stopped liking me? What if the phone stopped ringing? What if the boys stopped passing notes to me? What if. . . .? What if I wasn't popular next year, or the next, or the next? What if I lost the very thing that had defined my worth?

Sure enough, over time my worst fears were realized and my poplarity died down. I faced the humbling reality that the title of "most popular girl" was only for a season.

There were others waiting in the wings to replace me in the years that followed. At the time I was too young to question how one little contest and the resulting label of "most popular girl" could change the way people treated me. I mean, I was basically the same girl before being voted most popular, but my phone wasn't ringing off the wall when I was just plain ol' Vicki.

As I look back, I now see the covetous title of *popular* as more of a curse than an award. Why is popularity important to so many girls? Having been Miss Popular let me take a stab at answering that question. Many girls,

Everyone wants to be attractive, talented, and liked by others, but it gets out of balance when our worth becomes dependent on those things.

including me, define their worth and value by the world's equation:

Worth = What I look like + What others think + What I do

Now that I'm older, I realize that I had falsely based my worth on the equation above. If I didn't feel pretty, talented, or other people didn't like me, I didn't feel good about myself. Sure, everyone wants to be attractive, talented, and liked by others, but it gets out of balance when our worth becomes dependant on those things. The truth is, most popular people are living by the equation above. The sad part is that the very things they think will bring them worth and value will in reality leave them empty in the end.

In the process of molding themselves to the world's equation for worth and popularity, they begin to lose sight of who they really are and who they were meant to be. They are not true to themselves or to God.

If you struggle with wanting to be popular or you are popular, hide God's equation for worth in your heart:

Worth = What God thinks of me

You may not look like a supermodel, but in God's eyes you are remarkably and wonderfully made (see Psalms 139:14). You are his creation, and you are beautiful. The next time your reflection in the mirror begins to argue with that truth, smile and walk away. The next time you find yourself caught up by what others think, remind yourself of how God thinks of you. Once you have claimed Jesus Christ as your Savior, there is nothing you can do to make God not love you. Even at times when you are disobedient and unlovable, God still loves you. If that isn't a truth that causes your heart to swell with worth and value, then I don't know what will.

Notice that in God's equation, there is nothing related to "what we do." That's because it is impossible to win God's approval by good deeds. I've heard it

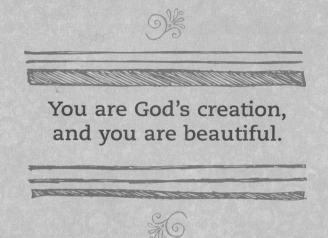

You are God's creation, and you are beautiful.

said that God loves us so much that if he had a wallet, our pictures would be in it. The truth is we are already popular—with the God of this universe! ✱

do you fit in?

a s a parent volunteer at my son's high school, I recently attended a meeting of about three hundred students. The meeting was for a student leadership organization that was given the task of voting for the homecoming theme. I watched with interest as students were given four choices for the theme and asked to raise their hands when their favorite theme was called. I watched a group of about eight to ten girls as they discussed among themselves which theme they would choose. When it came time for the vote and their preferred selection was called, they raised their hands in unison. As they glanced around the room, it quickly became apparent that their choice was not the popular choice. A few of the girls became visibly uncomfortable and quickly lowered their hands before their vote was counted. I turned to a fellow parent volunteer and said, "Bless their hearts, if they buckle so easily to peer pressure when it comes to the homecoming theme, they don't stand a chance when it comes to drinking, trying drugs, or having sex."

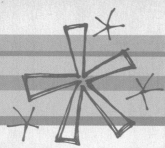

Most every teen wants to fit in. For the Christian teen, this will be a challenge, especially if fitting in means compromising their faith or values. It's only a matter of time before you are faced with either "fitting in" or "standing strong." Standing strong may come with a price and mean risking your place in the group. For three handsome teenagers in the Bible, it meant risking much more—their very lives.

Perhaps you remember the account of Shadrach, Meshach, and Abednigo in the third chapter of Daniel in the Old Testament. They faced the biggest challenge of their young lives when King Nebuchadnezzar issued a command for all people to fall down

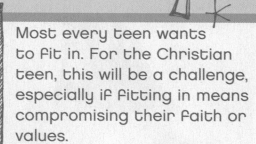

Most every teen wants to fit in. For the Christian teen, this will be a challenge, especially if fitting in means compromising their faith or values.

and worship a gold image he had created. This was not your average gold statue. It was ninety feet high! The cue to bow down was the sound of the horn, flute, zither, lyre, harp, pipes, and all kinds of music. Further, the king ordered that anyone who refused to fall down and worship the gold image would immediately be thrown into a blazing furnace (see Daniel 3:4–6).

Shadrach, Meshach, and Abednigo refused to bow down and worship the image. The king was notified of their disobedience, and they were summoned to come before him. He gave them one more chance to bow down and worship the golden image, and reminded them that should they choose not to, they would be cast into the fiery furnace. He further asked them, "Who is the god who can rescue you from my power?" (Daniel 3:15).

Now stop for a minute and think about their dilemma. It is human nature to want to conform, yet they overcame that temptation to bow down to the image the first time the song was played. What a picture to imagine the three young boys standing throughout the entire medley of music while everyone else had hit the dirt, most likely at the first blast of the horn. What a shame they were the only three. Would you have remained standing during the first playing of the song? I hope so. If you think you passed the test, hang on a minute. Now put yourself in their place the second time around. Are you still standing? Ouch. If it's human nature to want to conform, then it's all the more so to want to *live*.

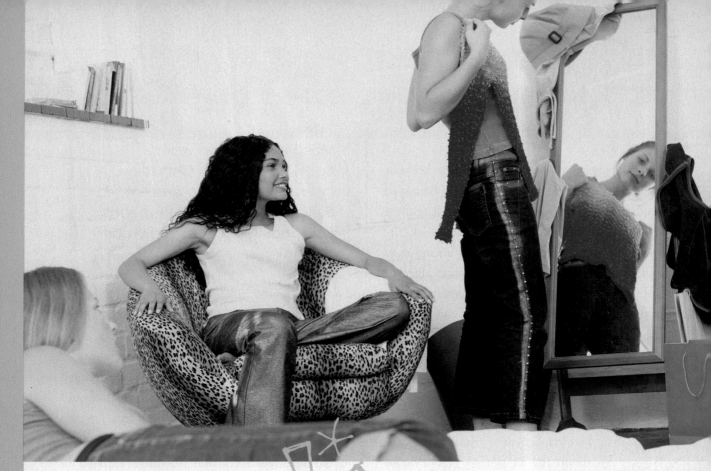

I love the boys' response to the king's command when he gave them a second chance to bow down and worship the gold image.

"Shadrach, Meshach, and Abednego replied to the king, 'Nebuchadnezzar, we don't need to give you an answer to this question. If the God we serve exists, then He can rescue us from the furnace of blazing fire, and He can rescue us from the power of you, the king. But even if He does not rescue us, we want you as king to know that we will not serve your gods or worship the gold statue you set up'" (Daniel 3:16–18).

Now, if that's not radical, I don't know what is. Forget the music and send the orchestra home. No need even to play a chord, these boys had made up their minds. Further, they knew their God was capable of rescuing them, but they did not have the foreknowledge to know whether he actually would. They were prepared to die for God, rather than reject him by bowing down to an idol. Most of us,

had we made it through the first song still standing, would have complied with the king the second go-round after taking one look at the fiery furnace.

King Nebuchadnezzar was so angry with the boys' response that he ordered the fire in the furnace be turned up seven times hotter than normal. In fact, the furnace was so hot that the soldiers who threw the boys into the furnace were killed by the flames.

> **Don't copy the behavior and customs of this world, but let God transform you into a new person by changing the way you think. Then you will know what God wants you to do, and you will know how good and pleasing and perfect his will really is.**
> (Romans 12:2 NLT)

Of course, there is a happy ending to the boys' story when they were brought out of the furnace

girl talk

QUICK beauty tips

You've probably heard your mom say that "beauty comes from the inside" and thought "Yeah, right Mom, tell the guys that." Well, believe it or not, your mom is right. So, what really makes a girl attractive? Try these beauty secrets:

SMILE: If you haven't discovered this "face-lift for free," try smiling more often. It will brighten your entire face.

EYE CONTACT: Make direct eye contact when you are speaking with someone. When you nervously avert your eyes, it makes you look insecure.

VOICE: Does your voice sound confident and mature? Some girls carry their "baby talk" voice into their adult years, and it is not attractive. Believe it or not, the maturity of your voice and your ability to carry on a conversation will be of critical importance when it comes time for you to find a job.

POSTURE: When I was your age, my mother used to tell me constantly to quit slumping my shoulders and to stand up straight. It drove me crazy . . . until I saw a picture of myself and was horrified! It made me look so insecure that I started making a concentrated effort to pull my shoulders back and stand taller.

COMPASSION: If someone is hurting, do you make an effort to speak words of compassion to them? A simple "I'm sorry you're going through that. Is there anything I can do to help?" goes a long way and most important, reveals the beauty in your heart.

OUTWARD FOCUSED: If a friend shares a difficulty with you or expresses sadness over something, do you remember to ask them how they are doing the next time you see them? It may even merit a phone call or e-mail to check on them.

SERVANT'S HEART: I am shocked at the number of people who have never been taught to look out for the needy. I have watched teenagers brush past elderly people practically knocking them over when heading through a door. If you see someone in need, elderly or not, offer to help them. A servant's heart is one of the most beautiful character qualities there is.

THE WAY YOU TREAT YOUR PARENTS AND SIBLINGS: There is nothing more unattractive than a girl snapping sarcastically at her parents or her siblings in public. If this is a problem for you, learn to hold your tongue and express yourself when the time is right.

ABILITY TO LAUGH AT YOURSELF: Have you learned to laugh at yourself when you do something embarrassing? Everyone is going to blow it from time to time whether they trip and fall, or say something totally idiotic. Rather than act paranoid, crack up! If you don't make a big deal of it, chances are no one else will either.

ABILITY TO ADMIT WEAKNESSES OR FLAWS: Everyone has weaknesses—it's a fact. Can you admit to yours when they show up or do you pretend like you always have your act together?

REJOICE WITH THOSE WHO REJOICE: Very few people (including Christians) can sincerely be happy when others around them succeed. However, those who rejoice when others rejoice display their beauty for all to see.

ATTITUDE: Have you noticed how your attitude can affect an outcome? You can't always change your circumstances, but you can choose your attitude.

CONFIDENCE: There is a big difference between being confident and being conceited. Confidence comes from being sure of yourself because you appreciate the gifts God has given you. Conceit is when you have a high opinion of yourself and take the credit for your giftedness.

BE YOURSELF: Most teens will knock themselves out trying to conform to the culture around them and the preferences of others. Rare is the girl who is truly authentic and comfortable with herself. Don't be a pretender. You are a unique creation of God.

FAITH: A girl who loves Jesus more than life can't help but shine from the inside out. She will brighten every room she enters, and her glow for Christ will be contagious. *

Do you crave attention? Maybe you regularly cast yourself as the center of attention, and you don't even realize it. Take the quiz to find out.

Are You an Attention Junkie?

A friend calls you and excitedly tells you she is going snow skiing over spring break. You went to the same place a few years ago. You:

a) let her finish and, when the time is right, tell her that you have been to the same place.

b) immediately interrupt her and scream, "I've been there!" and turn the conversation to your trip.

You are at cheerleading practice, and everyone on your team is going on and on about how the new girl can do a back with a full. You just did it last week and they weren't there to see it. You:

a) join in and agree that her full is incredible, knowing they will see yours in due time.

b) tell them that you got your back full last week at open gym.

When you are in a group of friends, you:

a) usually take part in the conversation by allowing others fair time to speak.

b) usually dominate the conversation and often interrupt others with your viewpoint or comments.

You are shopping for new school clothes. When you are trying on an outfit, you find yourself:

a) wondering if it is something that looks like "you."

b) thinking more about whether or not others will be impressed.

You are with a couple of your friends, and they mention a party coming up, and ask you if you got invited. You didn't. You:

a) express your disappointment but don't dwell on it.

b) go on and on to your friends about how no one likes you. You are baiting for empathy.

If you answered (b) two or more times, you need to take a serious look at your need for attention. Make a concentrated effort to catch yourself before interrupting others, dominating the conversation, baiting for empathy or compliments, and practice refraining. You may think no one has noticed, but rest assured, they have.

girl talk

Issues
of the
Day

ONE LITTLE DRINK

My youngest son accompanied me recently to a speaking engagement in Alaska, and we stayed a few extra days to take in the sights. On our first day my son saw a moose out in the wild. On our second day, he saw a whale out in the open ocean. On our third day he saw a bald eagle soaring high in the open skies. And on our fourth day he saw a drunken fool stumbling around at a patio restaurant.

Yep, we were eating dinner at a sidewalk café, and a woman at a table nearby was putting on quite a show. She was talking loud, slurring her words, and could hardly stay in her chair. When she got up to leave, her friends took her car keys from her and helped hold her up as they walked her to the car. We watched as she swayed back and forth, many times almost taking her friends down with her. It was quite a sight. My son and I tried to keep from laughing at her foolish display.

Later I found myself wondering if this woman had any clue just how ridiculous she looked when she finally sobered up. It made quite an impact on my young son, and I made a point to take advantage of the teachable moment. I told him that what he witnessed was the outcome of what can happen when someone drinks in too much. "Think about that," I told him, "should you find yourself tempted someday."

One of the greatest temptations you will face in your teen years is the temptation to drink alcohol. In one survey of teens, nearly one-third of seniors reported having at least five drinks in a row in the previous two weeks.[1] "Binge" drinking means having five or more drinks on one occasion. About 15 percent of teens are binge drinkers in any given month. Many teens admit that they were caught completely off guard the first time they were faced with the temptation to drink. The peer pressure to have "one little drink" can be tremendous. You

many teens admit that they were caught completely off guard the first time they were faced with the temptation to drink. You would be wise to come up with a plan before you are faced with the temptation.

would be wise to come up with a plan before you are faced with the temptation. Of course, the sheer fact that drinking is illegal should be enough to cause you to lay off the liquor. Unfortunately, this does not appear to deter some teens, so let me give you some other reasons to say no to drinking alcohol:

• **According to a Gallup poll, 25 percent of Americans say drinking is a problem in their home. Do you want to carry a drinking problem into your adult years that will impact your future family?**

• Mixing alcohol with medications or illicit drugs is extremely dangerous and can lead to accidental death. It is estimated that 25 percent of emergency room admissions may be due to alcohol-medication interactions.[2]

• **One drink can make you fail a breath test. In some states people under the age of twenty-one who are found to have any amount of alcohol in their systems can lose their driver's license, be subjected to a heavy fine, or have their car permanently taken away.**

- Most teens aren't drinking alcohol. Research shows that 70 percent of people ages twelve to twenty haven't had a drink in the past month.[3]

- **Drinking alcohol affects your brain by causing a loss of coordination, poor judgment, slowed reflexes, distorted vision, memory lapses, and possibly, blackouts.**

- Alcohol can damage every organ in your body. It is absorbed directly into your bloodstream and can increase your risk for a variety of life-threatening diseases, including cancer.

- **Alcohol affects your central nervous system, lowers your inhibitions, and impairs your judgment. Drinking can lead to risky behaviors, including having unprotected sex.**

- One study has shown that 60 percent of young adult women who are infected with a sexually transmitted infection report that they were under the influence of alcohol at the time that they had sex with the infected person.[4]

- **Alcohol is the #1 date-rape drug.[5]**

- Drinking large amounts of alcohol can lead to coma or even death. Over one-third of traffic deaths of fifteen- to twenty-year-olds were alcohol related.[6]

Come up with a plan today—don't wait another minute. Decide what you are going to say when someone pressures you to take a drink. It's only a matter of time before it happens. If you are ever at a party where alcohol is present, leave at once, even if it means leaving alone. You may get some ribbing from your friends, but in the end, who needs friends like that? And whatever you do, don't ever get in the car with anyone who has been drinking. You may not live to regret it. ★

> ## Don't get drunk with wine, which [leads to] reckless actions, but be filled with the Spirit. (Ephesians 5:18)

1. Federal America's Children 2001 report as reported in the Austin American Statesman by Kathleen Parker, *Orlando Sentinel*, 21 July 2001, "Good Times, Bad Times for Children in America."
2. H. D. Holder, "Effects of Alcohol, Alone and in Combination with Medications" (Walnut Creek, CA: Prevention Research Center, 1992).
3. 1998 National Household Survey. (SAMHSA), see http://www.health.org/gov pubs/ph323.
4. See http://teenadvice.about.com/library/weekly/aa121901a.htm.
5. See http://www.vanderbilt.edu/alcohol/daterape.html.
6. Fatality Analysis Reporting System, National Highway Traffic Safety Administration, 1998.

the secret shame

While sexual abuse may be an unpleasant subject to discuss, it is necessary, given its prevalence in our culture. Approximately one in three girls is sexually abused before the age of eighteen.[1] If that's not shocking enough, approximately one in four girls is sexually abused before the age of fourteen.[2] It only gets worse by college as one in four college women have either been raped or suffered attempted rape.[3]

Considering that about one-third of the girls reading this have experienced the secret shame of sexual abuse, I want to speak very candidly to you about this topic. Even if you are one of the fortunate ones who has not experienced sexual abuse, chances are you will encounter someone who has experienced the secret shame and carries a heavy burden. Whether this information is for you or someone else, here are some critical things you need to know:

Even though certain factors can encourage or invite sexual abuse, there is never an excuse for taking advantage of someone against their will. For example, alcohol, drugs, or clothing of a revealing nature may be factors that invite unwanted sexual advances, but this does not excuse the behavior of the abuser. I have had many girls cry on my shoulder and say something to the effect of "I had too much to drink, and I kept saying stop, but he wouldn't. I guess I probably deserved it." No one deserves to be abused—ever. While some girls may have made poor choices leading up to the abuse, they did not make the abuser abuse them. The abuser made the choice to sin. Yet many girls will carry guilt for years and blame themselves.

If you or someone you know has been sexually abused, talk to your parents or someone at your church. Ask them to help you or your friend take the next step in finding a reputable Christian counselor. The pain of sexual abuse is very complicated, and in most cases professional help is needed to begin the healing process.

If you or someone you know is currently being sexually abused, get help immediately. Do not wait

Whether you are on a date or simply find yourself in a precarious situation, learn to say, "I'm not comfortable with that." I hear from so many girls who tell me they just "didn't know what to say."

I cannot emphasize the importance of telling someone who can assist you or your friend in finding proper help. The sooner the healing process begins the better. It is never wise to carry the pain of sexual abuse into a future marriage. ✳

another moment. Find someone you trust and tell them. I have counseled grown women at events who have confided that they experienced sexual abuse in their past but had never told anyone. Stuffing painful events from your past deep down inside is not emotionally healthy. Often it will surface in the future through negative behaviors. The bravest thing you can do is tell someone who can assist you or your friend in getting help.

Therefore, no condemnation now exists for those in Christ Jesus. (Romans 8:1)

Therefore, no condemnation now exists for those in Christ Jesus.

(Romans 8:1)

1. Jim Hopper, Child Abuse: Statistics, Research, and Resources (www.jimhopper.com/abstats).
2. Ibid.
3. Ibid.

IS GAY OK?

maybe it's just me, but I'm sick and tired of the gay agenda in Hollywood. I'm tired of seeing a gay guy prancing around on just about every prime-time show. I'm tired of watching Madonna and Britney lip lock on TV. And I'm tired of having the "gay is OK" message shoved in my face by the liberal forces in this country. Whew, I feel so much better now that I've said that. When I was your age, a show like *Will and Grace* would be the talk of the town. And if someone like Will had come to my conservative Texas hometown and displayed his flamboyant out-of-the-closet gay pride—well, let's not even go there. Trust me, it wouldn't be pretty.

I recently spoke to a large youth group on the topic of moral relativism and the tolerance movement. As an example of the gay agenda, I pointed out to the youth how shows like *Queer Eye for the Straight Guy* and many others glamorize homosexuality as hip and cool. I warned the youth that while they may think these shows are funny and harmless entertainment, there is a clear agenda among the producers of the show to push the "gay is OK" message to viewers with the long-term goal of making homosexuality an acceptable behavior in the minds of their viewers. After my talk I was approached by a guy in the youth group who thought I went way overboard in condemning shows with flamboyant gay characters. He went on to say that no one he knows really thinks it's OK to be gay. I politely disagreed with him and told him that surveys are showing that more and more people are beginning to view homosexuality as an acceptable behavior, with the highest percentage being among teens. This is not a coincidence. For example, in a Barna survey of over one thousand people, 30 percent of all adults surveyed viewed homosexuality as "a morally acceptable behavior." That's almost one-third of the adult population in the United States! If that's not shocking enough, among the adults surveyed who were identified as "born again Christians," 20 percent viewed it as "a morally acceptable behavior." The largest percentage (40 percent) who viewed homosexuality as morally acceptable, were the youngest adults surveyed (eighteen to nineteen years old).[1] It is no coincidence that more and more young adults are finding the behavior acceptable given the time and attention it gets on television and through other media outlets.

And lest you think for a minute that your generation is not being influenced by the media when it comes to attitudes toward homosexuality, you might want to talk to a mom I visited with a few days ago. She was very distraught over the fact that her eleven-year-old daughter's best friend had French-kissed another girl at a sleepover during a game of Truth or Dare. We have Madonna and Britney to thank for making a "lesbian kiss" appear chic and acceptable. But don't be fooled! These girls will have to deal with the shame for the rest of their lives when the reality of what they did begins to sink in.

I also hear countless stories of teens who are badgered in school for implying or stating that homosexuality is "wrong." The tolerance movement, which basically puts a stamp of acceptability on anything but Christianity, has gotten way out of hand. In fact, if you even speak out against homosexuality, you are often labeled as a homophobic. This has always amused me because homophobic actually means a "fear of homosexuals." Those of us who have the boldness to speak up and say, "Hey, it's wrong," are certainly not afraid of homosexuals. Of course, we need to make sure that our words are laced with grace and kindness.

I am also disturbed by the vast number of lies that are told in schools around the country implying

that homosexuality is determined by genetic factors. No solid scientific evidence exists today that supports that people are born as a homosexual. In other words, scientists have not located a "gay gene," therefore homosexuality is not born or biological. This is not to say that some people are not predisposed to homosexuality. It is not any different than being predisposed to alcoholism or depression, yet notice that neither of these conditions is embraced as healthy or acceptable. Rather we encourage people who act out on these tendencies to find relief

> In Romans, homosexual behavior is referred to as **"sinful,"** a **"sexual impurity,"** **"degrading,"** **"shameful,"** **"unnatural,"** **"indecent,"** and a **"perversion."**

and recovery. Why should homosexuality be treated any differently? Especially, given the fact that the Bible, our ultimate guidebook for living, is very clear on the issue of homosexuality. Here is what it says:

Therefore God delivered them over in the cravings of their hearts to sexual impurity, so that their bodies were degraded among themselves. They exchanged the truth of God for a lie, and worshiped and served something created instead of the Creator, who is blessed forever. Amen.

This is why God delivered them over to degrading passions. For even their females exchanged natural sexual intercourse for what is unnatural. The males in the same way also left natural sexual intercourse with females and were inflamed in their lust for one another. Males committed shameless acts with males and received in their own persons the appropriate penalty for their perversions (Romans 1:24–27).

In the Romans passage above, homosexual behavior is referred to as "sinful," a "sexual impurity," "degrading," "shameful," "unnatural," "indecent," and a "perversion." There are other verses as well that leave no doubt that homosexuality is a sin according to God. I find that many Christians who are wishy-washy on their attitudes toward homosexuality are not always aware of what God said in his Word regarding homosexuality.

My comments may sound harsh but my sincere goal is to present you with the truth. Many issues we are currently facing in our country have to do with attitudes about homosexuality. Christians must not remain silent on this issue any longer. We must not be afraid to say, "Homosexuality is wrong," but we must be careful to do so in a spirit of love and grace. With humility, we must learn to love the sinner and hate the sin, remembering that we too, are sinners saved by God's grace. ✱

> *"For all have sinned and fall short of the glory of God."* (Romans 3:23)

1. See www.Barna.org.

Is God Pro-life?

Did you know that almost half of American women (43 percent) will have an abortion sometime in their lifetime? Abortion was made legal in 1973, and in the three decades that have followed, more than forty-four million abortions have been performed. Let me put that into perspective for you. Had those forty-four million unborn babies been carried to term, they could fill two states the size of Texas. In one year alone, more children died from abortion than Americans died in the Revolutionary War, the Civil War, World Wars I and II, the Korean War, the Vietnam War, and the Gulf War combined.[1] What must God be thinking about the casual way we discard our preborn? Psalm 139 leaves no question that God values human life from the moment a child is conceived.

> **For it was You** who created my inward parts; You knit me together in my mother's womb. I praise You, because I have been **remarkably** and **wonderfully** made. Your works are wonderful, and I know [this] very well. My bones were not hidden from You when I was **made in secret**, when I was formed in the depths of the earth. **Your eyes saw me** when I was formless; all [my] days were **written in Your book** and planned before a single one of them began.
>
> (Psalm 139:13–16)

Ninety-three percent of all abortions occur for social reasons (i.e. the child is unwanted or inconvenient). Essentially, what this boils down to is that those who have abortions are not willing to sacrifice nine months of "inconvenience" in order to allow their own child an entire lifetime. There is no shortage of couples who desperately want children and cannot have them.

When I was your age, I believed that abortion must be acceptable because it was legal. I was taught that the fetus is nothing more than a mass or blob of unrecognizable tissue. Many of my friends and I bought this lie when we were your age. We were not taught the truth about fetus development in the womb. And sadly, many from my generation and the generations that followed went on to have abortions. Do not be mistaken; abortion is not a quick-fix solution to an inconvenient problem. If teen girls could see the number of adult women who have cried on my shoulder over the guilt they still carry from a past abortion, they would know it is anything but a quick fix. Carrying a child is one of the greatest miracles from God. It is impossible for a woman to terminate a pregnancy and not experience emotional consequences at some point. Many of these consequences surface years later when the reality of what they have done begins to sink in.

Because abortion has become so common in our society, I want you to know the truth regarding fetal development should you or one of your friends ever face the reality of an unplanned pregnancy.

FACTS ABOUT FETAL DEVELOPMENT[2] (keep in mind that week 6, is about two weeks after a missed period)

WEEK 6 The embryo is about one-fifth of an inch in length. A primitive heart is beating. Head, mouth, liver, and intestines begin to take shape. **WEEK 10** The embryo is now about one inch in length. Facial features, limbs, hands, feet, fingers, and toes become apparent. The nervous system is responsive, and many of the internal organs begin to function. **WEEK 14** The fetus is now three inches long and weighs almost an ounce. The muscles begin to develop and sex organs form. Eyelids, fingernails, and toenails also form. The child's spontaneous movements can be observed. **WEEK 18** The fetus is now about five inches long. The child blinks, grasps, and moves her mouth. Hair grows on the head and body. **WEEK 22** The fetus now weighs approximately one-half pound and spans about ten inches from head to toe. Sweat glands develop, and the external skin has turned from transparent to opaque. **WEEK 26** The fetus can now inhale, exhale, and even cry. Eyes have completely formed, and the tongue has developed taste buds. Under intensive medical care the fetus has over a 50 percent chance of surviving outside the womb. **WEEK 30** The fetus is usually capable of living outside the womb and would be considered premature at birth. **WEEK 40** This marks the end of the normal gestational period. The child is now ready to live outside of the mother's womb.

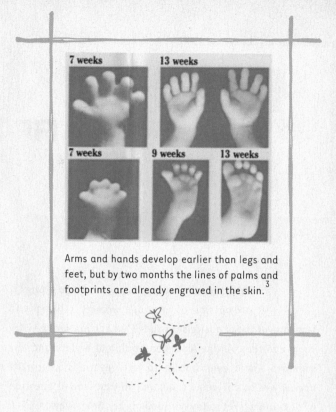

Arms and hands develop earlier than legs and feet, but by two months the lines of palms and footprints are already engraved in the skin.[3]

Given this information, it's amazing that 55 percent of teens view abortion as "morally acceptable."[5] My guess is that they have never been told the truth. Will you help me tell them? Your efforts could help save a life. ✱

Carrying a child is one of the greatest miracles from God. It is impossible for a woman to terminate a pregnancy and not experience emotional consequences at some point.

Most abortions are not performed until nine weeks of the pregnancy. Even RU 486 chemical abortions can't be done until after six weeks. By that time the baby has identifiable arms and legs (day forty-five) and displays measurable brain waves (about forty days). During the seventh through the tenth weeks, fingers and genitals appear, and the child's face is recognizably human.[4]

1. See http://www.nrlc.org/abortion/facts/abortionstats.html; stats for 2000.
2. John Dworetzky, *Introduction to Child Development*, 6th ed. (San Francisco, CA: West Publishing Company, 1996), 70–75 (www.w-cpc.org/fetal.html).
3. Ibid.
4. See http://www.liferosary.com/facts.htm.
5. See http://www.barna.org/FlexPage.aspx?Page=BarnaUpdate&BarnaUpdateID=152.

RIGHT IS RIGHT AND WRONG IS WRONG

IS homosexuality wrong? Is gay marriage wrong? Is sex outside of marriage wrong? Is living with someone of the opposite sex wrong? Is abortion wrong? Fifty years ago the average American would not understand why someone would even bother to ask questions where the answer was so obvious. I think we call that kind of question a "no brainer." Yet today our thinking has been skewed. Even Christians struggle to brand certain behaviors as wrong. We live in a culture that preaches political correctness. Many

outside the womb is killed when passing through the birth canal. Trust me; I am sparing you from the gory details related to how that baby is killed. Does it get any worse than this? I fear it will.

But see, here lies the danger of a culture that allows each individual to define their own standards for right and wrong. A nation grounded upon a system of moral relativism that believes what may be right for one person may be wrong for another and vice versa. This type of skewed thinking

> We live in a culture that preaches political correctness. Many Christians remain silent, not wanting to make waves or risk offending anyone.

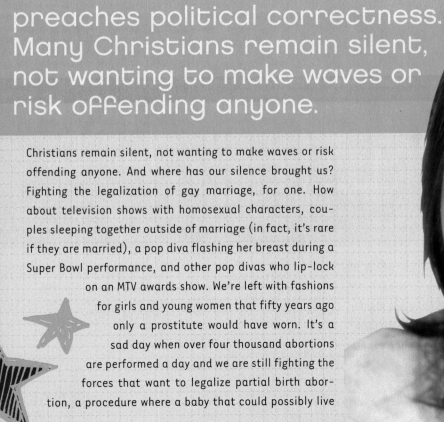

Christians remain silent, not wanting to make waves or risk offending anyone. And where has our silence brought us? Fighting the legalization of gay marriage, for one. How about television shows with homosexual characters, couples sleeping together outside of marriage (in fact, it's rare if they are married), a pop diva flashing her breast during a Super Bowl performance, and other pop divas who lip-lock on an MTV awards show. We're left with fashions for girls and young women that fifty years ago only a prostitute would have worn. It's a sad day when over four thousand abortions are performed a day and we are still fighting the forces that want to legalize partial birth abortion, a procedure where a baby that could possibly live

spouse? Marry someone under age? Terminate a pregnancy because the ultrasound showed it was not the sex a couple preferred? Use aborted fetuses for research purposes? Smoke marijuana or do other drugs in the privacy of their homes? It's only a matter of time because there are people today who honestly believe some of the issues mentioned above are right and should be legal. It is a slippery slope, and it will only get worse unless we fight moral relativism.

Let's go back to the now famous Madonna and Britney kiss on the MTV awards show. Do you know what Madonna had to say about it after the show? "We're bored with the concept of right and wrong." So now Madonna is making up the rules for her version of "right and wrong" and making us watch her doomed experiment on live television. Clearly she finds nothing wrong with making out with another woman. What amazes me is that the outcry was over the lesbian kiss, but there were other disturbing issues associated with the kiss that got overlooked. How about the fact that she is a married woman and her husband sat on the front row and watched as his wife planted one on Britney (and Christina). Would we have made a big deal about it if this married woman kissed a man? Probably not, but we should. What about the fact that Britney and Christina are young enough to be Madonna's daughters?

> A nation grounded upon a system of moral relativism . . . believes what may be right for one person may be wrong for another and vice versa. This type of skewed thinking leads to an "anything goes" type of society.

leads to an "anything goes" type of society. Correct me if I'm wrong, but wasn't Sodom and Gomorrah an "anything goes" type of society? If you've never heard of it, don't bother looking it up on a map—God torched it long ago, and archeologists are still finding the ashes to prove this Old Testament account. I am certainly not suggesting that God is planning a similar demise for the USA, but there is no mistaking that our country is in a moral freefall. If Christians don't come out of their silent cocoons and find the boldness to speak up and say "Enough!" I cringe at the thought of where we will find ourselves in fifty more years. Our grandparents would never have guessed we would be facing some of the issues we face today. Fifty years from now, will you be shocked when it is legal for people to have more than one

Ick. That's just gross if you think about it. And what about the fact that Madonna is a mother? In fact, Madonna's six-year-old daughter, Lourdes, performed on stage at the same MTV awards show while her mom sang "Like a Virgin." Little Lourdes was dressed in First Communion white, decked out in lace gloves, a crucifix, and a studded belt with the words "BOY TOY." Am I the only person out there who thought something was terribly wrong with that picture? News flash to Madonna: Little girls are not "boy toys" and should never be advertised as such. One reporter had this to say: "What kind of craven, twisted mother enlists her own daughter in such a shameless public orgy?" I tell you what kind of mother—the kind who is bored with the concept of right and wrong. The kind who will kiss someone young enough to be her daughter for the purpose of pushing her warped agenda down our throats. You would think there would be a public display of outrage in this country over Madonna's attempts to brainwash viewers with her doctrine of right and wrong. But no, instead we reward her behavior by putting her new children's book on the best-seller list within weeks of "the kiss." Again, am I the only one who finds it disturbing that parents are willing to support Madonna in her efforts to influence our children?

You may wonder why I am going over this issue in a book directed to Christian girls. How does the issue of moral relativism affect Christian teens who should know better than to believe that there is no absolute moral standard for

nearly identical to that of nonborn-again teens. Clearly we have a problem.

In one survey teens were asked the question, "When you are faced with a moral or ethical choice, which one of the following best describes how you, yourself, decide what to do?" They were given ten choices of which one was: follow a set of specific principles or standards you believe in, that serve as guidelines for your behavior: the Bible. Only 7 percent of teenagers surveyed answered they would look to the Bible when facing a moral dilemma. And get this: only 12 percent of born-again teenagers who were surveyed said they would look to the Bible. The most popular answer among teens, Christian and non-Christian alike was:

Right is right and wrong is wrong, and nothing will ever change that fact—even a culture who tries to change the rules to please themselves. In the end everyone will have to answer to a Holy God and explain their actions.

behavior? Surprisingly, a survey shows that just one out of ten born-again teenagers in this country believe in absolute moral truth, a statistic that is

whatever feels right or comfortable in that situation. Now that ought to scare us half to death. Think about it. If the majority of teens are making decisions based on what *feels* right versus what God says *is* right, you can bet that when faced with the temptation to have sex, teenage hormones will cast a vote to go for it. When faced with the temptation to drink, do drugs, cheat, lie, steal, curse, and so on, only a handful of teens are going to flip open their Bibles to see what God has to say about it. I have taught my kids the importance of choosing the kind of friends who, when faced with peer pressure or temptations, would choose *doing* good over *feeling* good. I told them that this means only about forty-two of the six hundred students in their class will look to the Bible when facing a moral dilemma. And get this: Out of the 150 students (most born again) in their youth group at church, only about eighteen will look to the Bible when facing a moral dilemma! So the next time you tell your mom and dad that so-and-so from your school goes to church and is a good kid, remember the survey.

Don't fall for the lie of moral relativism. God created an absolute standard of morality and gave us the Bible as the ultimate answer book. Right is right and wrong is wrong, and nothing will ever change that fact—even a culture who tries to change the rules to please themselves. In the end everyone will have to answer to a Holy God and explain their actions. I'll have plenty to answer for concerning myself, but I sure hope I'm not standing behind Madonna on that day. ✴

For you were once darkness, but now [you are] light in the Lord. Walk as children of light—for the fruit of the light [results] in all goodness, righteousness, and truth—discerning what is pleasing to the Lord. Don't participate in the fruitless works of darkness, but instead, expose them. For it is shameful even to mention what is done by them in secret. Everything exposed by the light is made clear, for what makes everything clear is light. Therefore it is said: "Get up, sleeper, and rise up from the dead, and the Messiah will shine on you." Pay careful attention, then, to how you walk—not as unwise people but as wise—making the most of the time, because the days are evil. (Ephesians 5:8–16)

Don't fall for the lie of moral relativism.

What Do You Believe?

Did you know that a large percentage of Christian youth end up renouncing their faith during their college years? Most of them are caught off guard when they enter liberal colleges and sit under professors who are openly belligerent to Christianity. I recall one of my professors at the University of Texas in a philosophy class who asked the Christians to raise their hands to identify themselves on the first day of class. A few students had the boldness to do so. The professor then proceeded to announce that one of his goals would be to expose the idiocy of the Christian faith and tear their belief system to shreds by the end of the semester. I was not a Christian at the time, so I laughed at his sarcastic comments along with the majority of the class (many of whom probably grew up in the church). Sure enough he remembered the students who had raised their hands and openly picked on them throughout the semester when the topic of discussion lent itself to Christian bashing. Are you ready to stand up for what you believe? First, you have to know what you believe.

1. All faiths worship the same God.

    True   False

2. Satan is not a real being but rather a symbol of evil.

    True   False

3. As long as you're a good person, you will go to heaven.

    True   False

4. The Bible was meant to be nothing more than a compilation of stories written by men.

    True   False

5. The Bible tells us that God helps those who help themselves.

    True   False

6. There is more support for the evolution position than the creation position.

    True   False

7. People who are gay cannot help it—they are born that way.

    True   False

8. Abortion is morally acceptable in certain situations.

    True   False

9. Embryos from aborted fetuses should be used for stem-cell research to help find a cure for certain disabilities.

    True   False

10. Truth can only be defined on a person-by-person basis and will vary from situation to situation.

    True   False

If you answered "True" to any of these ten statements, you have misunderstood the basic tenets of Christianity and are in danger of having a non-Christian worldview. If you missed any of the above questions, it would be a good idea to do a Bible study that addresses the basics of Christianity and what it is to have a Christian worldview. The issue of worldview is a very important one because your worldview (or view of the world) will determine your belief system, which in turn, will impact your actions. You can claim to be a Christian and embrace a worldview that contradicts the teachings of Christianity. Most importantly, read God's Word on a regular basis. The more you are in God's Word, the more familiar you will become with truth and fiction. ★

How Spiritual is the average teenager?

Nearly nine out of ten (89 percent) teens pray weekly. (1999)

Over half of teens (56 percent) attend church on a given Sunday. (1999)

Thirty-eight percent of teens donate some of their own money to a church in a given week. (1999)

Thirty-five percent of teens attend Sunday school in a given week. (1999)

Thirty-five percent of teens read the Bible each week, not including when they are in church. (1999)

More than seven out of ten teens are engaged in some church-related effort in a typical week: attending worship services, Sunday school, a church youth group, or a small group. (1999)

Thirty-two percent of teens attend youth group, other than a small group or Sunday school, each week. (1999)

Twenty-nine percent of teens attend a small group each week that meets regularly for Bible study, prayer, or Christian fellowship, not including Sunday school or a twelve-step group. (1999)

In 1997, 88 percent of teens say they are Christian. This number dropped to 82 percent in 1999. (1999)

Of those who call themselves Christians, 26 percent said they are "absolutely committed," and 57 percent said that they were "moderately committed" to the Christian faith. (1999)

Almost two-thirds of teens (62 percent) believe that the Bible is totally accurate in all of its teachings. (2000)

One out of every three teens (33 percent) is born again. (1999)

Three out of every five call themselves "spiritual" (60 percent). (1999)

Slightly more than half (53 percent) say that Jesus committed sins while he was on earth. (2000)

Almost two-thirds describe themselves as "religious" (64 percent). (1999)

Only 4 percent of U.S. teens are evangelicals. (1999)

Twenty-eight percent of teens feel a personal responsibility to tell others about their religious beliefs (56 percent of born-again Christian teens feel this way). (1999)

Fifty-six percent of teens feel that their religious faith is very important in their life. (1999)

Thirty percent of teens believe that all religions are really praying to the same God; they are just using different names for God. (1999)

Three out of five say they are "committed Christians" (60 percent). (1999)

Two out of three teens (65 percent) say that the devil, or Satan, is not a living being but a symbol of evil. (2000)

Three out of five teens (61 percent) agree that if a person is generally good, or does enough good things for others during their life, they will earn a place in heaven. (2000)

In total, 83 percent of teens maintain that moral truth depends on the circumstances, and only 6 percent believe that moral truth is absolute. (2001)

When it comes to believing in absolute truth, only 9 percent of born-again teens believe in moral absolutes, and just 4 percent of the nonborn-again teens believe that there are moral absolutes. (2001) ✶

: George Barna (www.barna.org/FlexPage.aspx?Page=Topic&TopicID=37).

My Child, Do You Remember Me?

My child, do you remember me?
We met so long ago.
You were formed inside my womb,
yet never allowed to grow.

My child, will you forgive me
for the life I stole from you?
Will you know the tears I've shed
for that child I never knew?

I never got to see your face,
or hold you in my arms.
I pray someday you'll understand
I never meant you harm.

I know you're in a better place,
and someday I'll meet you there.
For Jesus has forgiven me,
my sin, I no longer bear.

I missed playing peek-a-boo
and going to the park.
I missed holding you in my lap
when you were afraid of the dark.

My child, will you remember me
on that day we meet again?
Will you even know my face
or wonder where I've been?

I missed your pretty pictures
of rainbows in the sky.
I missed the cards on Mother's Day
the kind that make you cry.

"Yes Mother, I remember you;
we met so long ago.
Why I could not stay with you,
I really do not know."

I missed you learning to ride a bike
and your first dive into the pool.
I missed your every summertime
and your every first day of school.

"Now come with me and meet the Lord,"
my child will smile and say.
"I'll take your hand and lead you there,
for He'll wash your tears away."

I missed your every birthday
and watching you grow each year.
I missed saying "I love you"
and showing how much I care.

And finally, I'll approach His throne,
my sins as white as snow.
With open arms, my God will say,
"My child, welcome home."

—Vicki Courtney ©1995

Friends and Family

forever **friend** or

Who doesn't remember at some point singing the catchy tune, "Make new friends but keep the old; some are silver and the other gold"? Well, if there was ever a time to start singing it again, it is high school. One of the most difficult adjustments in high school is making friends, some of which will be

casual acquaintance?

of the twenty-four-karat gold variety and others more like the cheap gold vermeil that you get for a quarter in bubblegum machines. The tricky thing is that they both appear to be gold on the outside, but only one has what it takes to last over the years. So how can you tell the difference between solid-gold friends and the ones who shine about as long as those rings from the bubblegum machine?

Think about your friends as you look at the list below. Would they make the cut?

24k solid gold

• If you are sad, this friend will lend a shoulder to cry on. • Your secrets are safe with this friend; she has proven herself trustworthy. • If you are moody, this friend will give you space and not take it personally. • This friend would never consider liking the same guy you do or flirting with him behind your back. • This friend listens as much as she talks. • If you make plans with this friend, she would never ditch you for someone else, including the guy she likes. • This friend loves you for who you are, and you are free to be yourself around her. • If you were in a bind, you could count on this friend to help you out. • This friend watches your back and would come to your defense if necessary. • This friend is humble and willing to apologize when she is wrong. • This friend forgives easily and doesn't hold grudges. • This friend values your advice. • If you unexpectedly found yourself in a situation that was morally compromising, like a party where someone has alcohol, this friend would be the type to leave with you.

Do you have any friends like this? Better yet, are you the twenty-four-karat solid-gold type of friend? You will make many friends in your teen years. As you get to know them, remember that some are worth the investment of your time, while others are better left as acquaintances. Every girl deserves at least one friend that passes the twenty-four-karat test. **If you don't have a friend like that, pray and ask God to provide you with one.** If you do have a friend like the one described, treat her as precious as gold. She is a priceless treasure.

But it is you, a man who is my peer, my companion and good friend! We used to have close fellowship; we walked with the crowd into the house of God. (Psalm 55:13–14) ✱

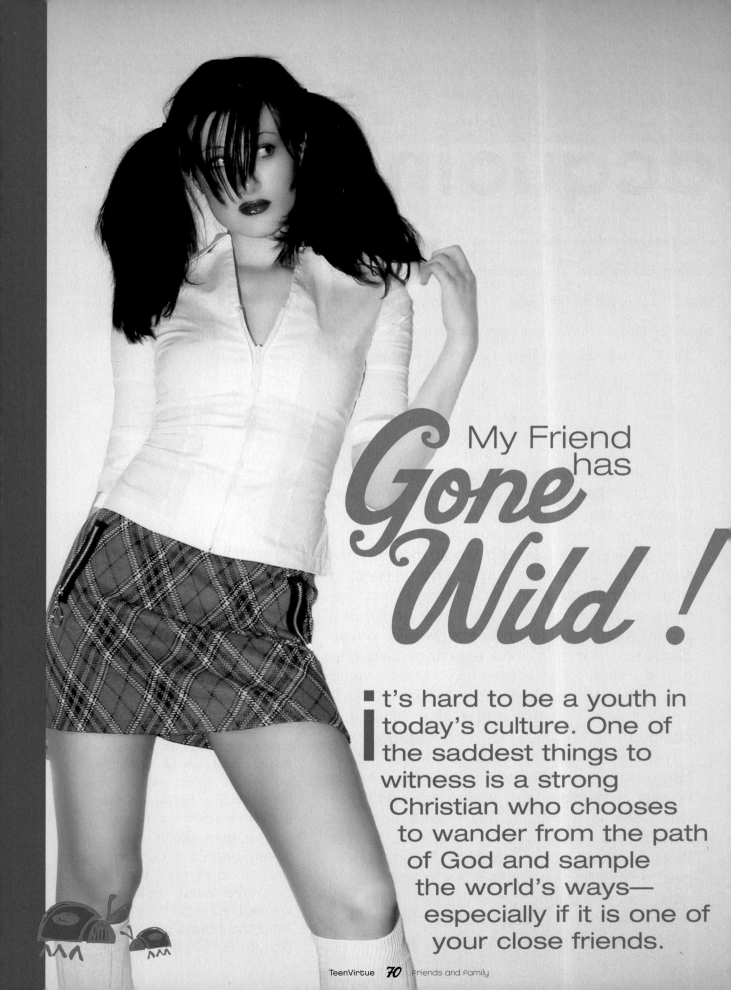

My Friend has Gone Wild!

it's hard to be a youth in today's culture. One of the saddest things to witness is a strong Christian who chooses to wander from the path of God and sample the world's ways— especially if it is one of your close friends.

Some years ago one of my friends announced that she was leaving her husband for another man that she had met. She and her husband were Christians, and she even led a weekly Bible study. Her husband was devastated and assured my husband and me that he had done nothing to justify a scriptural reason for divorce (adultery). He shared that he was saddened over the fact that many of his wife's Christian girlfriends accepted her announcement and appeared to be happy for her. No one likes confrontation, but c'mon! If her friends really cared for her, they would face their fear and say something before the couple became another painful divorce statistic.

Armed with this knowledge and a sincere concern for my friend, I gave her a friendly call and asked her if the rumor of the divorce was true. She responded by telling me that it was true and that she had "prayed about it and concluded that in the end God would want her to be happy!" At this point I gently (*gently* is the key word, here) confronted her and told her that God would never approve of two Christians divorcing when there was no scriptural reason. I further told her that it would not make sense for God to contradict his own teachings regarding divorce in the Bible, even for her own perceived personal happiness. I wish I could tell you that the story had a happy ending, but she ended her marriage, and she ended our friendship, as well. While I was sad, I knew that in the end I had acted more as a friend in confronting her in love than the others who stood by and said nothing or, even worse, affirmed her sinful choice.

You've probably figured out by now that church kids are not exempt from temptations to cheat, curse, drink alcohol, try drugs, or have sex. If you have a close friend who goes wild, it can be painful to stand by and watch her self-destruct. You are faced with a

difficult choice when it comes to continuing the friendship. If you are facing this situation, you have no other choice but to hold your friend accountable for her actions.

Not only is it a sign of true friendship to confront a friend who is making sinful choices; it is scriptural. Matthew 18:15 says, "If your brother sins against you, go and rebuke him in private. If he listens to you, you have won your brother." Before you attempt this, be sure to check your motives before God. If your motive is anything other than love and concern for your friend, do not go. Holding a close friend accountable must be done in a spirit of love, or it could drive your friend even further from God. Be honest in saying, "This is one of the hardest things I have ever had to do, and I have been praying about it for a while. I know you've been making some bad choices lately, and it makes me sad because I know that's not who you really are." If you begin by reminding her gently of her Christian faith and giving her the benefit of the doubt, it is more likely that you will disarm her from responding in

anger. She may even open up and share her heart with you. **Sin always leads to emptiness, and she could be dying inside over her bad choices.** If your friend responds in brokenness (a sadness over the fact that a heavy price was paid with Jesus' death on the cross for her sin) and repentance (a sincere desire to turn from her sin and change), respond with grace and mercy.

On the other hand, if your friend is defensive and refuses to change, tell her that

friend is still not responsive, you would be wise to limit your contact with your friend for a time. The last part of Matthew 18:17 says to "let him be like an unbeliever and a tax collector." The Israelites did not associate with Gentiles or tax collectors and considered them to be immoral people. This does not excuse you from treating your friend with kindness and praying for her. Make it a habit to check in with her from time to time and ask her how she's doing. There is no need for a sermon—your words of kindness will do more to bring her back to the path of God. An occasional phone call, IM, or text message will do wonders to remind her that she is loved by you and God, in spite of her unlovely behavior.

It is quite possible that your friend will not return to her Christian faith, and

> # Sin always leads to emptiness, and they could be dying inside over her bad choices.

you love her but will have to distance yourself from the friendship for awhile. I know this sounds harsh, but the odds are not good that you will be the one to change your friend. The truth is, you have little in common at this point. The rest of the passage in Matthew 18:16 says, "But if he does not listen to you, take one or two more with you, so that by the mouth of two or three witnesses every fact may be confirmed" (NASB).

Rather than involving some of your other mutual friends in the accountability process, I would talk to your youth minister first and suggest that he or she take the next step in talking with your friend. If your

like my case, the close friendship you once had will come to an end. This is a painful reality and should it occur, mourn the loss of your friendship and move on. Be faithful to lift her up in prayer from time to time as God brings her to mind. While it is not common, I have heard of cases where someone who has been held accountable by a close friend will make contact many years later to say "thank you." Regardless of the end result, rest in the peace that you showed genuine love for your friend by holding her accountable to the pain of sin. Besides, we don't serve others for the praises of men but to hear our Father say, "Well done." ✱

If you're in high school, you've probably experienced the frustration of having a best friend get a boyfriend. The time you once spent hanging out together must now be shared with someone else. If the relationship gets really serious, you may find yourself looking for a new best friend. This was my case when I got to high school and my closest friend from middle school discovered the world of dating. Within weeks of our freshman year, she went from one serious boyfriend to another for the next four years.

The relationship ended when we went to two separate colleges, and we haven't seen each other since. What a waste. What I would give to go back and do it all over again.

If I had it to do over, I would value and nurture my friendships, knowing they were more likely to last over the years than a relationship with a high school boyfriend. I envy some of my friends today who valued and nurtured their friendships in high school and still get together twenty or thirty-plus years later

WHEN YOUR BEST FRIEND /// GETS A BOYFRIEND ///

Sometimes she switched boyfriends out so fast, I wondered if she didn't have a wait-list going. Sure, I had a few boyfriends in my high school years, but I didn't really have a serious boyfriend until my junior year, so this all came as a shock to me as a new freshman.

Most girls enter high school assuming, like I did, that it will be a similar social situation to that of middle school. **They don't factor in that some of their friends will bail on their girlfriends when the first guy looks their way.** Once they are officially allowed to date—go out in a car with a guy—you may see them as often as you see that distant great aunt who stops in every few years to visit and can't tell you from your sister. It is a painful reality, and even though it may not seem right, there is little you can do to make her change. **Girls who invest the majority of their time during high school in serious dating relationships have a deeper problem.** They do not feel significant unless they "belong" to a guy and they spend their every waking minute together. They avoid being without a boyfriend because deep down inside it would make them feel undesirable. It doesn't matter how many girlfriends they have because they have falsely defined their worth and determined that they are worthless without a boyfriend.

If your friend has traded her time with you for a guy, the best thing you can do is to make sure you have other friends to hang out with. And remember, if you meet a guy and the relationship becomes serious, don't give up your girlfriends for the relationship. No guy is worth that, especially in high school. One of my biggest regrets in high school was that I gave up my girlfriends for a serious boyfriend in my junior and senior year. I wasted two years of high school in a joined-at-the-hip relationship that practically emulated marriage.

They do not feel significant unless they 'belong' to a guy.

for occasional girl trips. I forfeited my chances for close, life-long friendships for a guy I haven't seen since high school. Take a lesson from me and don't let that happen to you. Even if you end up being one of the rare few who goes on to marry your high school boyfriend, you will not regret maintaining your friendships. ✱

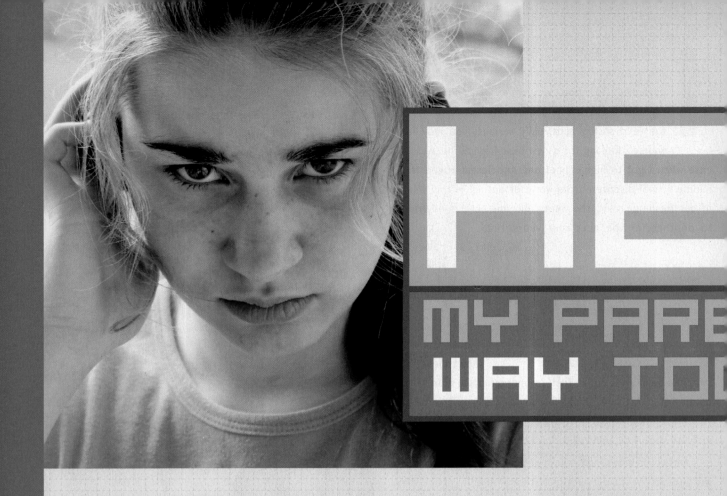

HE

MY PARE

WAY TO

When my oldest child began his freshman year in high school, I attended a parent orientation held by the school counselor. She had all the parents break up into small groups and asked us to answer the following question: "If there was one thing you wish your parents had done differently in your high school years, what would it be?"

Amazingly, seven of the eight parents in my group answered something along the lines of "I wish my parents had been more aware of what was going on in my life and had drawn more boundaries." I was one of them, and the general consensus was that it could have spared us some harsh consequences of having to learn some life lessons the hard way.

HELP
MY PARENTS ARE
STRICT!

While there is no way your parents can protect you fully from making poor choices, they should be aware of the dangers of the culture and set up some boundaries. Parents who are not engaged in their children's lives, by default, are allowing the culture to rear their children.

Now, I realize that most teens would prefer to have no set curfew, no one looking over their shoulder when they are IMing, no one asking questions like, "What did you do at the party," no one insisting on calling your friend's parents before the party to make sure they will be there, no one objecting to certain movies containing inappropriate material, and no one grilling them over homework assignments. Does that sound like a dream come true to you?

As a parent who cares about the well-being of my children enough to harass them about all of the above, let me assure you that it takes time to care. It would be much easier to just mentally check out and let the culture parent my kids. But it's not the right thing to do. I view my job as parent as a very serious calling and

I bet most of your parents do too. God has entrusted my husband and me with children who belong first and foremost to him. We have about eighteen years on average with each child to train them as best we can to live in the world without becoming of the world. This is no easy task, especially given the times. When teaching a child to swim, most parents don't throw him or her in the deep end and scream, "Sink or swim, it's your choice! Good luck!" Most parents will train their children step-by-step until they are ready to go it in the pool alone. It is the same thing with life training. God expects parents to efficiently use the eighteen years they have been given to adequately train their children before they strike out on their own.

So while you may think the kids whose parents have checked out are the lucky ones, remember, they will be the ones twenty-plus years from now wishing they had had your setup. My husband and I realize that we may not get a "Thanks, Mom and Dad!" from our children during their teen years, but one thing is for certain: When they attend their own child's freshman parent orientation, they won't be among the majority wishing their parents had been more attentive. Maybe then they'll call and say, "Thanks." ✱

> You may think the kids whose parents have checked out are the lucky ones . . .

There are "friends" who destroy each other, but a real friend sticks closer than a brother. (Proverbs 18:24 NLT)

Are You a Good Friend?

I overheard my daughter and one of her friends talking the other day. (Seriously, I wasn't eavesdropping—they were in the back seat of my car!) My daughter had mentioned a girl that was in her class, and her friend gave her a friendly warning to "be careful—she can be a backstabber." Wouldn't you die if others warned people about you?!

Take the following quiz and find out if you pass the test for being a good friend.

QUIZ:

You have plans to go to the game with your friends. A few days before the game, the guy you like asks you if you want to go with him. You . . .

a) tell him maybe next week but you already have plans. You never dump your friends for a guy.

b) tell your friends sorry—guys come first; especially the one you like.

You have a crush on one of your friend's boyfriends, and he starts to flirt with you online. You . . .

a) copy and paste his comments and send them on to your friend to warn her. The crush is officially over. Why would you like a guy that betrays his girlfriend?

b) flirt away—it's all harmless fun, right?

A friend starts to trash one of your other friends. You . . .

a) get your nerve up and tell her, "Hey, I like her." Case closed.

b) nod your head but don't say anything. You don't want to make waves.

One of your friends calls you and is really upset about a fight she just had with someone. You are about to leave to go to the mall and spend one of the gift cards you got for your birthday. You . . .

a) drop your plans to go to the mall and head over to your friend's house.

b) console her over the phone as best you can and then offer to call her later when you get home from the mall.

Your best friend gets invited to a party that you wanted to go to but you didn't get invited. You . . .

a) are hurt, but you don't let her know. You want her to have a good time and not worry about you.

b) whine and complain to her until she feels guilty for getting an invitation.

If you answered (b) one or less times, you are an awesome friend. Bravo, way to go, friend.

If you answered (b) two or three times, you may want to brush up on your friendship skills. Make an effort to think of others before yourself.

If you answered (b) four or five times, you need to do some serious soul-searching. If you're not willing to change, you may want to get a gerbil to keep you company on the weekends. Your friends won't put up with your friendless ways for long. ★

Make an effort to think of others before yourself.

I Give My Mom an E for "Embarrassing"

I remember a time when I was a teenager and my mom was the designated driver in charge of carting my friends and me to the mall. I sat there sweating it out, wondering if she could make it the full five miles without embarrassing me. As she pulled up in front of the mall, I breathed a huge sigh of relief thinking I was going to escape the car embarrassment-free. But then she did it.

As my friends and I were exiting the car giggling with high energy, she shook her head back and forth and said, "Oh to be so young and gay." Later I tried to patiently explain to her that while *gay* may have meant "happy" in her day, it meant something entirely different in mine. Of course, my friends thought it was hilarious, and I never heard the end of it. They would often chant my mom's words back to me at school, all in fun. While it was beyond embarrassing at the time, today I find it cute and funny. It's amazing how becoming an embarrassing mom can cause you to gain a whole new perspective about your own embarrassing mom. Now, I know that it's hard for you to imagine that, as cool as you are right now, your future children might someday label you an "embarrassment." Heaven forbid, you might even marry a man who mows the lawn in black dress socks.

Take it from this mom—we don't set out to embarrass you on purpose. We may joke that our mission in life is to embarrass you, but it's just a cover-up for the inevitable. The truth is, we just can't help it. We are totally and completely out of touch with your world. And it's probably a good thing. You don't really want a mom who is trying so hard to be in touch with your world that she dresses like you and your friends, talks like you and your friends, and wants to hang out with you and your friends. If given a choice, you probably want a mom who acts like a mom.

Now I realize that some of you have legitimate complaints when it comes to your mom embarrassing you. I remember moms who would scream at their daughters in the presence of others, tease them about liking a certain boy, criticize them for what they were wearing, or even sing out loud to songs on the radio while in the car (unforgivable, especially if they are your songs). I have a flashback of my mom driving and singing, "My baby takes the morning train" at the top of her lungs while my friends and I sat in the back seat and prayed for the torture to end. But seriously, if your mom embarrasses you more often than not, think about sitting her down and sweetly telling her. Most moms are reasonable people who can likely remember back to their own growing-up years when they had an embarrassing mom.

Leviticus 19:3 says: "Each of you is to respect his mother and father." When your mom embarrasses you, resist the temptation to lash out at her in front of your friends or treat her, with disrespect. Wait for the right time to talk with her and then sit her down and let her know how her comments or actions made you feel. Chances are, if you treat her with respect, she will treat you with respect in return. Now, does this guarantee that she'll stop parading around the house in those goofy brown loafers and white crew socks? Not a chance. ✱

> Take it from this mom, we don't set out to embarrass you on purpose.

R U ALIVE?

10 TIPS ON SURVIVING GIRL POLITICS

Let's face it, girls can be mean. If you haven't experienced some level of girl politics by now—jealousy, gossip, cliques, and mean girls—then you've likely never been to a middle school sleepover with an uneven number of girls. Throw in some popcorn and you've got yourself a show . . . or better yet, a showdown.

Chances are you've been on both the giving and receiving end of girl politics. Girl politics is nothing new. Ask your mom—I bet she can share a story or two about girl politics that she suffered when she was your age. Even the Bible is chock-full of girl politics. Wherever there has been more than one woman present, girl politics have been present.

> **Even the Bible is chock-full of girl politics. Wherever there has been more than one woman present, girl politics have been present.**

Girls who dole out their poison through girl politics are no different from the male school-yard bully except they leave bruised hearts instead of black eyes. Many victims find themselves in therapy years later, paying $90 an hour to untangle the web of emotional damage. The new wave of reality shows has brought about a new breed of blatant in-your-face criticism. This speak-your-mind, tell-it-like-it-is trend has

taken the definition of *mean* to the next level. Not to mention, technology has enabled mean girls to spread their venom electronically with the click of a mouse. So, if we can't avoid it, what can we do about it? Below are ten survival tips that, if put into practice, can help safeguard you from girl politics.

1. Remember, you are who you hang out with. If you hang out with girls who gossip, talk ugly about others, and leave girls out on purpose, chances are good that you have been dubbed one of the "mean girls" at your school. **Choose your friends wisely. If you want to avoid girl politics, don't hang with girls who have made it their favorite hobby.**
DO NOT BE DECEIVED: "BAD COMPANY CORRUPTS GOOD MORALS."
(1 Corinthians 15:33)

2. If you are on the receiving end of girl politics, do not escalate the situation. If you are the victim of a mean girl, remember the instigator is provoking you to get under your skin. If she doesn't succeed, chances are good that she will move on. Don't even give her a minute of your time and energy. Treat her as though she was invisible.
HOW HAPPY IS THE MAN WHO DOES NOT FOLLOW THE ADVICE OF THE WICKED, OR TAKE THE PATH OF SINNERS, OR JOIN A GROUP OF MOCKERS!
(Psalm 1:1)

Remember, you are who you hang out with. If you hang out with girls who gossip, talk ugly about others, and leave girls out on purpose, chances are good that you have been dubbed one of the 'mean girls' at your school.

I realize that I may lose you on this next one, but the Bible tells us to "pray for those who mistreat you." It's a radical concept, and few Christians will succeed in loving their enemies, much less praying for them. God knew that the best remedy for healing our own hurt feelings is to take the focus off ourselves. When we pray for others who hurt us, it keeps bitterness from taking root in our hearts.

"LOVE YOUR ENEMIES, DO GOOD TO THOSE WHO HATE YOU, BLESS THOSE WHO CURSE YOU, PRAY FOR THOSE WHO MISTREAT YOU."
(Luke 6:27–28)

Know the difference between a clique and a peer group.

A clique is defined as a narrow circle of persons associated by common interests or for the accomplishment of a common purpose. The definition goes on to state that it is generally used in a bad sense.

A clique is any group that purposely excludes others and acts as if they are better than everyone else. The average clique usually includes one to two strong-willed girls who are the ringleader(s) and a number of other girls who are the followers. Many sweet girls are lured into cliques because they have falsely defined their worth and base their worth on the superficial acceptance of the group. Of course, no clique is complete without one or more targeted victims. Woe to the poor girls who unwillingly become the designated victims. The best way to protect yourself is to avoid cliques at all costs.

On the other hand, a peer group is safe. Most girls will gravitate toward girls they have things in common with. This is normal, and there is nothing wrong with having a preference for some friends over others. When you were younger, your mom probably made you include all the girls in your class to avoid hurt feelings. As you get older, this becomes more unrealistic. The key is to be kind to everyone. Never close the door to new friendships. You may discover you have common interests with someone who is not in your peer group.

SO FOLLOW THE WAY OF GOOD PEOPLE, AND KEEP TO THE PATHS OF THE RIGHTEOUS.
(Proverbs 2:20)

If you often find yourself on the receiving end of gossip, don't be flattered. It means that they find you a willing party and a fellow gossiper. If you make clear that you are not comfortable participating in gossip, it won't take long for your friends to figure it out. No one wants to share tasty tidbits with someone who won't play the gossip game. If you don't want to gossip but can't figure out a way to tell your friends without sounding preachy, try telling them, "I always feel bad after I gossip, so I'm trying to do better." That way you put the problem on yourself while making clear that you don't want to take part in gossip any longer.

A GOSSIP'S WORDS ARE LIKE CHOICE FOOD THAT GOES DOWN TO ONE'S INNERMOST BEING.
(Proverbs 18:8)

LIFE AND DEATH ARE IN THE POWER OF THE TONGUE, AND THOSE WHO LOVE IT WILL EAT ITS FRUIT.
(Proverbs 18:21)

Remember that anyone who readily shares gossip with you will readily share it about you with others. I have witnessed gossip separate more close friends when one party trusted the other with their secrets. Never trust anyone who gossips with something you don't want others to know, no matter how close a friend she is. If you are not getting along, what's to keep the other person from spilling your beans?

A GOSSIP GOES AROUND REVEALING A SECRET, BUT THE TRUSTWORTHY KEEPS A CONFIDENCE.
(Proverbs 11:13)

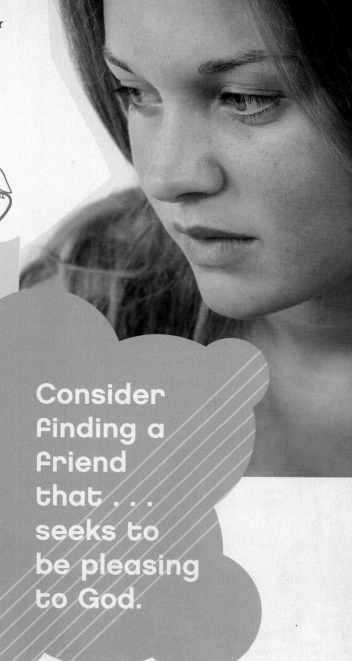

A true sign that a person feels good about herself is her ability to take joy in the successes of others. Rare is the girl who is confident enough in herself that she can sincerely be happy for another girl when she succeeds in something that the other girl had wanted for herself. The next time someone achieves something that you desperately wanted for yourself or gets asked out by the guy you like (ouch) or gets an award for something and you didn't, make an effort to celebrate with her. If you don't feel like it, act yourself into the feeling. The more you practice rejoicing with others and celebrating their successes, the more of a habit it will become.

REJOICE WITH THOSE WHO REJOICE; WEEP WITH THOSE WHO WEEP.
(Romans 12:15)

Consider finding a friend that . . . seeks to be pleasing to God.

Remember the general rule: People who make fun of others are extremely insecure. They somehow rationalize that if they point out the flaws of others, they will feel better about their own feelings of inferiority.

DO NOTHING OUT OF RIVALRY OR CONCEIT, BUT IN HUMILITY CONSIDER OTHERS AS MORE IMPORTANT THAN YOURSELVES.
(Philippians 2:3)

Avoid groupthink. Groupthink is when you conform to the group's point of view in order to stay in favor with the group. Many girls will go against their better nature and gang up on other girls because the group is doing so. They are too insecure to stand up for what is right.

HATE EVIL AND LOVE GOOD.
(Amos 5:15a)

10 Consider finding a friend that also seeks to be pleasing to God in the area of girl politics and agree to hold each other accountable. It's as simple as trading an e-mail once a week and checking in on each other. You should both agree in advance what you want the other person to ask you on a consistent basis. For example, if you struggle with participating in gossip, ask your friend to ask you each week if you have gossiped about someone or listened to gossip. When you know that someone is going to be lovingly checking in on you, you will be more likely to hold your tongue. Most importantly, agree to pray for each other. *

THEREFORE ENCOURAGE ONE ANOTHER AND BUILD EACH OTHER UP AS YOU ARE ALREADY DOING.
(1 Thessalonians 5:11)

All About Guys ♂ ♂ ♂ ♂

SOLVING THE
Male Mystery

I remember when my friends and I were your age and we would sit around and analyze for hours what we thought some certain guy meant when he said such and such. Was he flirting? Did he like me? Is he going to ask me out? Should I call him? In these girl talk sessions each and every syllable the guy had uttered was dissected for further research and study. We almost always cracked the code of what the guy in question actually meant—or so we thought. If worse came to worse and we were still left without a clue by the end of our sessions, we resorted to the tried-and-true get-your-friend-to-ask-him method.

At the time my friends and I had no idea that on the flip side, the guys were totally and completely clueless. Of course, we imagined that they also sat around and parsed through our words and flirtatious signals in a desperate attempt to crack the code of

ALL ABOUT
GUYS

the female mind. In reality, nothing could be further from the truth. Imagine a guy calling one of his friends and saying, "After class she said, 'maybe I'll see you later.' Do you think she said that because she wants to see me later, or did she just say it like it was no big deal with the emphasis on maybe?" As a mother of a typical teenage son, I have been given a glimpse into the world of guys. Ryan and his friends are cute, athletic, and fun to be around. In a nutshell they are the kind of guys girls sit around and talk about.

So, what do guys do in their free time? Let me give you an idea. Recently, I was returning home after running a few errands. I pulled up in front of my house just in time to witness my sixteen-year-old son sailing down the hill of our driveway on a rolling office chair. Now let me point out that this is not your average driveway. Our driveway is about 125 feet long and has a steep downhill slope from the top to the bottom. My son was picking up speed while grabbing the bottom of the chair and screaming for his life. His intended target was a skateboard ramp at the bottom of the driveway, and beyond the ramp was a pile of cardboard boxes, no doubt to help cushion his fall. His friends stood by cheering him on as they awaited their turn. (You would surely think they would change their mind after watching him.) As I watched my son travel down that driveway at rocket speed, launch off the ramp, and

crash into the boxes, I sat in my car dumbfounded. I was relieved to see him finally get up and limp back up the hill so he could, no doubt, get in line to try it again. It was at that very moment that it hit me: All those years that my friends and I sat around talking about guys, this was the kind of stupid stuff they were doing. Yes, these are our future leaders. Join me in a word of prayer.

Now don't get me wrong—they talk about girls, but it's usually short and sweet. Just like when you talk to them on the phone—no drama, just the facts. I made a comment to my son a few days ago about one of his best friends going out with a certain girl. I had found out about the "new couple" from his friend's mother when we went out for coffee. My son was totally clueless when I brought it up. He said something like, "Yeah, I guess that's why I've been seeing them together at school a lot." I replied by saying, "This is one of your best friends. Don't you guys talk about anything?" to which he replied, "Mom, we're guys, and guys don't talk about stuff like that." So there you have it. While you and your friends are sitting around trying to solve the latest cryptic guy puzzle, they are busy rolling down steep driveways on office chairs. And they say girls are more mature. . . . Imagine that. ✱

. . . they talk about girls, but it's usually short and sweet.

ALL ABOUT GUYS

FOUR TYPES OF DATING TO AVOID

AVOID AVOID AVOID AVOID AVOID

1 DATING FOR FUN

Girls should avoid going out with someone simply for the sake of saying they are going out with someone. Going out (dating) should not be the forum to explore initial feelings of attraction. Often in high school relationships begin based on nothing more than an initial physical attraction. Dating should never be entered into lightly. Build friendships and spend time in group settings where you are free to be yourself and get to know each other over time.

ALL ABOUT GUYS

2 DATING BY EMOTION

Most teen girls enter into dating relationships based on feelings more than facts. They rationalize that if it *feels* right, it must *be* right. Proverbs 4:23 provides a word of caution: "Guard your heart above all else, for it is the source of life." Part of guarding your heart will be learning to trust God more than your emotions. God would not want you to give your heart away prematurley by swapping casual proclamations of "I love you" in a relationship that years later will most likely be nothing more than a faded memory with "ol' what's his name."

Girls who follow their emotions when it comes to dating are more likely to follow their emotions when it comes to sexual temptations. Hormones will often send a message that if it feels right it must be right, and many will give in sexually because they believe it is the next step in the relationship. Additionally, the culture readily preaches feelings as a litmus test for determining readiness to have sex. You may feel ready to have sex, but that doesn't change the fact that sex outside of marriage is wrong.

3 "JOINED-AT-THE-HIP" DATING

Many dating relationships evolve into serious, long-term relationships that, in reality, emulate marriage. Often a couple will give up time previously spent with friends in order to spend more time together. Girls especially are attracted to dating relationships that emulate marriage because of their natural desire for romance and love. This type of "joined-at-the-hip" relationship almost always leads to physical intimacy due to the amount of time spent together. I am amazed at Christian mothers who facilitate this sort of relationship by allowing their daughters to spend too much time alone with their boyfriends. I realize that there are some serious Christian dating relationships among high school students who are mature in the faith that remain innocent and sexually pure, but they are the exception, not the rule. I have openly shared with my two older children my regret of having been involved in a serious "joined-at-the-hip" dating relationship for over two years of my high school years. We spent almost every waking moment together, swapped proclamations of love and eventually gave up our virginity for each other. Even though I was not a Christian, I knew in my heart that sex outside of marriage was wrong. Nevertheless, I justified it because it seemed the next step in a marriage-like relationship. Of course, like so many high school romances, the relationship ended within months of going our separate ways in college.

> EVEN THOUGH I WAS NOT A CHRISTIAN, I KNEW IN MY HEART THAT SEX OUTSIDE OF MARRIAGE WAS WRONG.

4 "MISSION FIELD" DATING

SOME CHRISTIAN GIRLS ATTEMPT TO JUSTIFY DATING NON-CHRISTIAN BOYS AS A WAY TO BE A WITNESS . . .

Woe to the young lady who compromises her Christian faith, much less, the faith of another, to date a young man who is not a Christian! Second Corinthians 6:14 cautions against Christians being yoked together with unbelievers (NIV). While the Scripture warns specifically of unequally yoked relationships in marriage, it should be remembered that most marriages are preceded by a dating relationship. If the principle is followed in dating, it could spare you much heartache should the relationship lead to marriage. I am amazed at how many Christian girls (and guys) ignore this verse because it would prohibit them from going out with someone who makes their heart beat faster. Many girls innocently enter into dating relationships with non-Christians because they are unaware of 2 Corinthians 6:14. Decide in advance not to date someone who is not a committed Christian.

Some Christian girls attempt to justify dating non-Christian boys as a way to be a witness and possibly lead them to faith in Jesus Christ. While it is possible for a Christian girl to lead her non-Christian boyfriend to Christ without her Christian standards being compromised in the process, it is rare. I witnessed a youth speaker illustrate this point by asking a student to stand on a chair. The student represented the Christian in the dating relationship. He then asked another student to come and stand on the ground next to the chair and for the two to clasp hands. The student on the ground represented the non-Christian in the dating relationship. The youth speaker asked the student on the chair to attempt to pull the other student up onto the chair, while the other student was told to attempt to pull the Christian student down onto the ground. It doesn't take a rocket scientist to figure out how this experiment ended. Am I suggesting that it is wrong to have guy friends who are not Christians? No way. Friends are one thing, but boyfriends are quite another. You will be a more effective light for Christ if you are not tangled up in a relationship with someone who does not know Christ.

When it comes to dating, girls should go before God in prayer well in advance of the "going out" stage and ask him for the wisdom needed to come up with a set of standards for dating. If you don't have a standard, you will most likely embrace the world's standard when it comes to dating. *

ALL ABOUT GUYS

the Truth about Prince Charming

My high-school-aged son recently experienced torture of the worst form. He and his friends made plans to attend a movie. Nothing unusual about a night at the movies unless, of course, you let the girls choose the movie. You got it—he was forced to endure two hours of the latest chick flick. When he got home, he wore a dazed and confused expression, similar to the kind you get when someone tells you a really lame joke and attempts to explain the punch line over and over again as they wait expectantly for you to laugh. Here is my son's review of the chick flick:

Dream about Prince Charming all you want, but don't be fooled. There's not a guy out there that will be able to complete you.

"Mom, I just didn't get it. The whole movie led up to this guy and girl getting together at the end. He goes through all this stuff to prove his love for her, and then he has to chase her down at the end to tell her. Give me a break—like a guy would really go to all that trouble to tell a girl he likes her. Trust me, any girl that puts a guy through all that automatically goes on the psycho list."

Bless his confused and insensitive heart! I then patiently explained that seven dollars is a small price to pay to view the world as it should be. The fairy tales, the chick flicks, and the romance novels cater to a woman's need to be noticed, pursued, rescued, and eventually won over by the world's most charming man. The perfect man will solve all of life's problems and bring us the happiness we long for—a happiness that won't come until or unless we find him. Only then will we crack the code to true love. If and when we find him, we will be forever changed—or so we are led to believe.

Ever notice how the chick flicks always end on an unrealistic high note? With the kiss time stands still. And there it ends, and we are left to imagine the happiness that follows. Of course, they get married, and she stares adoringly at him. They go on picnics in the park, and she stares adoringly at him. They run hand in hand on the beach, and she stares adoringly at him. Yeah, right! Can you imagine what the future might look like if the movie continued with a realistic picture of what would follow for most couples? He forgets to put the toilet seat down, channel surfs, belches, scratches, and leaves his dirty socks on the floor for her to pick up. Do you still think she's staring adoringly at him? No way! She's slappin' him upside the head and making

him sleep on the couch! What? You don't like reality? Well, that's the reason we have chick flicks—so we can get our romance fix and return to reality. Now this is not to say that marriage is never romantic. A good marriage will have its moments of romance, but even the best of marriages won't emulate the chick flicks.

The chick flicks do get one thing right. **We crave a brand of love that is lasting, perfect, and unfailing. Believe it or not, God placed that craving in our hearts.** Proverbs 19:22 says, "What a man desires is unfailing love." His ultimate goal was that the craving to find perfect love would lead us to the only one who dispenses it—Jesus Christ.

One of my favorite passages of Scripture is Ephesians 3:17–19. It says: "And that the Messiah my dwell in your hearts through faith. [I pray that] you, being rooted and firmly established in love, may be able to comprehend with all the saints what is the breath and width, height and depth, and to know the Messiah's love that surpasses knowledge, so you may be filled with all the fullness of God."

The word *filled* in this verse is derived from a Greek word, *pleroo*, that means to "complete" or "fill to the brim." Dream about Prince Charming all you want, but don't be fooled. There is not a guy out there that will be able to complete you.

Don't fall for the fairy tale any longer. No mortal man can offer you a brand of love that will quench the desire in your heart to be loved perfectly and completely. No one can love you with the love of God. Only when you allow Jesus Christ to take his rightful place in your heart will you find true love, and that's no fairy tale.

. . . and then she met her one true Prince and lived happily ever after. The End. ✳

surviving a heartbreaking breakup

Recently I was in a large bookstore and stumbled upon a section of books for teen girls. One book in particular that caught my eye made a startling claim on the front cover. The book claimed to contain spells that, if cast properly, would turn any ex-boyfriend into a toad. Now, while this Wicca tool is ridiculous and downright laughable, I couldn't help but wonder how many girls had snapped it up in the hopes that it just might work. After a bitter break up, many girls would rather picture their ex-boyfriend as a beady-eyed amphibian who spends his days slurping down flies and hopping from lily pad to lily pad. It beats facing the inevitable and unpleasant reality of seeing him walk down the halls of your school arm in arm with another girl.

Although it's been many years, I can still remember my first breakup. I wondered if I would make it though a single day without thinking of my ex-boyfriend. Would the pain ever go away? It was so tempting to pick up the phone and call or drive by his house. The first time I saw him with another girl, I could hardly breathe. It felt like my already broken heart had been ripped out of my chest and bulldozed a thousand times over.

As the years went on, I would experience more breakups. It didn't matter if I was the one breaking up or the one being broken up with—it was always painful. The longer the relationship had lasted, the harder it was to be apart and adjust to dateless weekends. But I survived, and you will too. I would have given anything to have had a formal survival guide to help me get through the lonely weekends. So before you consider the toad spell, check out the survival tips on the next page.

> ## Would the pain ever go away?

surviving a breakup 101

1. Don't fall for the "let's try to be friends" speech. Many times the promise to be friends is made to lessen the blow of a full-fledged, cold-turkey break-up. While it may seem a reasonable solution at the time, only in rare instances will a couple be able to return to the days of being casual friends. Woe to the poor girl who sacrificed her purity in the relationship. God created sex and sexually related activity as an expression of love solely between a husband and a wife within the confines of marriage. If exercised outside of marriage, it creates an emotional bond between the couple that is not easily broken when the relationship ends. The odds of being friends after a breakup with someone you have been intimate with are slim to none. Even in relationships where sexual intimacy was not a factor, it will be difficult to return to your prerelationship friendship.

2. Limit your contact. Resist the urge to call him, IM him, send him a text message, or e-mail him. If you have to, remove him from your buddy list so you won't be tempted to try to talk to him when you see him online. Don't checkup on him through mutual friends or purposely show up where he is working. It will take longer for your heart to heal when you purposely place yourself in his path in an attempt to prolong the inevitable.

3. Find things to take your mind off the breakup. Get together with friends and family. See a movie, go shopping, read a good book, or try out some new recipes in the kitchen. The more you engage your mind with other interests, the less you will think about him.

4. Resist the urge to get back together. I recall one relationship I had in college where breakingup and getting back together became a weekly routine. What a waste of valuable time! Why do girls cave in so easily? If you are tempted to get back together, remind yourself of all the reasons the breakup occurred in the first place. If it helps, make a list and keep it handy. Getting back together doesn't solve the previous problems, and it only prolongs the inevitable. When the breakup occurs again, you start all over in your healing process. It is emotionally draining to float in and out of a doomed relationship.

> Remember that God is the great Comforter.

5. Dwell on your one perfect love. When you find your mind drifting back to the pain of the breakup, pick up your Bible and read the Psalms. Talk to the Lord throughout your day, and tell him exactly how you feel. Remember, he is no stranger to rejection and heartache. Write down Scriptures that speak of God's perfect and unfailing love, and take them with you wherever you go. Make it a habit to camp out in God's Word daily. It will lift your spirits and give you a peace that surpasses all understanding.

Breakups take a toll on your emotions. Go into it knowing it is a process. Go easy on yourself and don't expect overnight results. Girls who follow God's standards for purity in a dating relationship will heal faster should the relationship come to an end. When you date someone, you invest a part of yourself in that person. It only makes sense that you would feel a sense of loss when a breakup occurs. **Above all, remember that God is the great Comforter. Fortunately, he's only a prayer away.** *

CAUTION: LOSER ALERT

WOULDN'T IT BE GREAT IF THE GUY YOU LIKED CAME WITH A WARNING LABEL, POINTING OUT HIS SERIOUS FLAWS?

Just as many people decide not to smoke based on the clear warning label that doing so may cause cancer, girls could decide up front whether or not dating certain guys poses a serious risk to their physical, emotional, or spiritual health. Of course, some girls are so blinded by love (or what they perceive to be love) that they would find a way to justify just about anything from "anger management issues that may lead to mass murder" to "you will never measure up to his ex-girlfriend so don't even try."

Over the years of doing events for young women and women, I have listened to many sad stories from countless high school and college girls, not to mention adult women, about the "loser" they are dating, dated at one point, or in some cases, ended up marrying. In most cases there were clear-cut warning signs that had they just seen them on the front end before entering the relationship; it may have saved them the heartache they were experiencing in the present. **And before you mistakenly assume that Christian guys can't fall into the loser category, let me assure you they can.**

ALL ABOUT
GUYS

In every case, the biggest mistake that the girls and women made was in making the assumption they could somehow change the glaring faults of the guy in question. Of course, in the end, they discovered the hard way that only God can change a willing heart. So what are the warning signs of a loser in the making? I will list the most serious character flaws below. Some will be obvious from the outset, while others may not become apparent until the relationship has progressed. They are serious enough that should you notice them in a guy you are considering dating; put the brakes on and put it in reverse. Don't even think about moving forward. If you are dating a guy and he exhibits any of the character flaws below as the relationship progresses, terminate the relationship at once. Believe me when I say that these character flaws will likely produce devastating fallout in the years to come should you continue in the relationship. **The list is not comprehensive, so know up front that the most important gauge you possess in determining which types of guys to avoid is the still, quiet voice of the Holy Spirit.**

WARNING! Avoid contact with any guy who displays one or more of the following character flaws. Do not pass go, do not collect $200, scram, flee, run for your life, get outta here!

I. A DESIRE TO CONTROL OR MANIPULATE

For among them are those who worm their way into households and capture idle women burdened down with sins, led along by a variety of passions, always learning and never able to come to a knowledge of the truth.
(2 Timothy 3:6–7)

Flee fast from the guy who seeks to control you through manipulation and mind games. **Do not consider it flattery to be the center of someone's life.** The center of our lives should always be Christ. I dated a guy in college who was overly jealousy of any guy who would talk to me. At first I thought it was endearing and cute, but after a few months it got out of hand. He became suspicious of my every move and made ridiculous accusations, always assuming I was steps shy of betraying him.

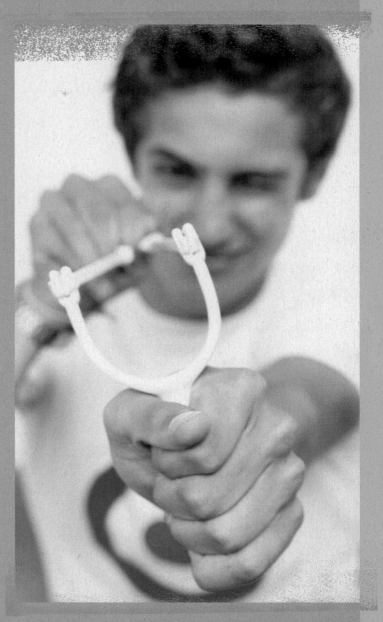

When will girls realize that jealousy and control are not flattering? The irony is that some girls assume that if a guy is infatuated with them, it is a good sign and proves they have some powerful force over a guy that leaves him crazy with obsession. In truth, this guy is not infatuated with the girl—he is infatuated with the idea of controlling the girl. **A guy will only seek to control someone he perceives to be controllable.** It is the guy with the power, not the girl. Girls who

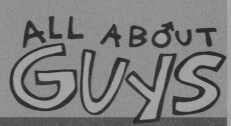

come out of this type of relationship suffer from a loss of worth and esteem. Jealousy, control, obsession, and manipulation are common forms of emotional abuse.

2. A TENDENCY TO BECOME EASILY ANGERED OR VIOLENT

An angry man stirs up conflict, and a hot-tempered man increases rebellion.

(Proverbs 29:22)

When I finally ended the relationship with the guy I dated during my college years that was controlling and manipulative, he reacted by putting his fist through the door in my apartment. I was fortunate that he didn't hurt me, but I have no doubts that it would have eventually led to him physically abusing me had I stayed in the relationship. He was so controlling that he stalked me in the months that followed. He would call and make threats to hurt any guy he saw me out with in the future. It got so bad that my

parents moved me out of my apartment before the lease was even up and moved me into a condo complex with a gated entry and high security.

I was fortunate that he finally grabbed a clue and left me alone, but it took me months to recover from the emotional damage. Some girls are not so lucky. One girl made the headlines in Austin, Texas when she was murdered by her ex-boyfriend after he became enraged when she broke up with him. They started off as the "cute couple" at their high school. She was a cheerleader, and he was a football player, and they seemed the perfect match to many. But it didn't take long for his true nature to emerge. The warning signs were all there. Her friends and family repeatedly warned her about his attempts to control her and his jealous tendencies. They told her that they worried it might eventually escalate to physical abuse. Unfortunately, it escalated to death. **Why did she ignore the obvious warning signs and the repeated warnings from her friends and family?** We may never know, but my guess is, she somehow justified his behavior because she rationalized that his obsession with her was a sign of his love. Love does not seek to control. Love does not harm. Love does not murder.

3. A PAST RECORD OF CHEATING

Whoever is faithful in very little is also faithful in much, and whoever is unrighteous in very little is also unrighteous in much.

(Luke 16:10)

Woe to the poor girl who dates a guy who has a past record of cheating on his previous girlfriends. Many girls who date cheaters justify that they will be the one girl to capture this guy's heart and his eyes will never wander again. Yeah, right. Unless he recognizes that he has a problem with commitment and has sought help for it, it is only a matter of time before she is in the same shoes as his last girlfriend. And do not be fooled for a minute—a guy who messes around behind his girlfriend's back will often mess around in marriage, so double woe to the poor girl who marries this type of guy and rationalizes his cheating habits away. **I have watched entire Christian families destroyed when the husband is caught carrying on with one of his wife's friends, another woman in the church, or a coworker.** Girls are just as susceptible to stray, so it would not be fair to place the entire blame on the guys. Some people crave the thrill that comes with sneaking around in secret. Unless they recognize that this is a problem and do something about it, it will continue to be a problem. Do not let this type of guy convince you that you will be the one girl who will make him faithful; he probably said the same thing to his last few girlfriends.

4. A TENDENCY TO THINK ONLY OF HIMSELF

Do nothing out of rivalry or conceit, but in humility consider others as more important than yourselves.
(Philippians 2:3)

Beware of the narcissist. A narcissist is defined as "a person who has love for his own body." A narcissist will always find a way to turn the attention or conversation to himself. It is always about him. Even when he is clearly wrong, he will avoid assuming responsibility and find a way to turn it into "poor me for having to put up with all this."

Narcissists are prone to addictive behaviors of every sort including alcohol, drugs, porn, online gaming, gambling, poker, spending money, and others. Because they are extremely selfish and self-centered and have determined that life is all about them, they rationalize their addiction(s) as something they deserve. They feed their pleasures

at the expense of others. Most narcissists, unless they repent and change, are incapable of having close, intimate relationships with others, yet many will marry if they can find someone who will tolerate and excuse their selfish behaviors. Often narcissists are charming, handsome, and confident. They are used to getting attention and have come to expect it. This type of guy looks for a girl who has a low self-esteem and will allow life to be all about him. Many girls will fall prey to this type of guy because they are initially attracted to his apparent self-confidence. Unfortunately, self will be the center of his life while the needs of others around him are ignored.

For people will be lovers of self, lovers of money, boastful, proud, blasphemers, disobedient to parents, ungrateful, unholy, unloving, irreconcilable, slanderers, without self-control, brutal, without love for what is good, traitors, reckless, conceited, lovers of pleasure rather than lovers of God, holding to the form of religion but denying its power. Avoid these people!
(2 Timothy 3:2–5)

> OFTEN NARCISSISTS ARE CHARMING, HANDSOME, AND CONFIDENT. THEY ARE USED TO GETTING ATTENTION AND HAVE COME TO EXPECT IT.

5. A PREOCCUPATION WITH COARSE JOKING OR SEXUAL TALK, SEX, LUST, OR PORN

But sexual immorality and any impurity or greed should not even be heard of among you, as is proper for saints. And coarse and foolish talking or crude joking are not suitable, but rather giving thanks.
(Ephesians 5:3–4)

We live in a time where it is nearly impossible to escape inappropriate sexual imagery. Many of our grandparents lived an entire lifetime and never once encountered what we encounter today in our e-mail in-boxes or uninvited pop-up ads. Teens create online profiles laced with sexual talk and

THEY HAVE A TENDENCY TO VIEW GIRLS AS "OBJECTS" RATHER THAN PEOPLE . . . DO NOT TAKE ANY CHANCES WITH THIS TYPE OF GUY.

coarse joking and make it available for all on their buddy list to see. As a mom who regularly checks profiles of my kids and the friends they have on their buddy lists, I am horrified by what I find sometimes coming from the "Christian" kids! Clearly these teens have assumed that all parents are electronically challenged. Television shows, movies, and music speak openly of sex outside of marriage, homosexuality, and other sinful behaviors that were at one time never discussed in private, much less in the open. **Vulgarity and crudeness have reached a whole new level.** And with it we are seeing record numbers of teenage boys and men addicted to online porn and chat rooms. A friend of mine who is a counselor specializing in sexual addictions said he has a waiting list a mile long of teenage boys and men seeking help for their problem. How sad. What's even sadder is that my friend also told me it is perhaps one of the hardest, if not the hardest, addictions to overcome. Many of these teenage boys will carry their problem into marriage.

I can guarantee you that your parents can count on at least two hands the families they know personally (even in church) who have been destroyed by this addiction. Because this is affecting teenage guys in mass

ALL ABOUT GUYS

numbers, including Christian guys, you need to steer clear of guys who exhibit an obsession with coarse joking or sexual talk, whether through IM or in person. The more they are exposed to sexual imagery, the more comfortable they become in making sexual references. They have a tendency to view girls as objects rather than people and often obsess over physical features. **Do not take any chances with this type of guy, even if he is a Christian and acknowledges the problem.** With a willing heart that is broken and repentant, change is possible, but it will take time and effort. DO NOT stick around for the healing process. You can be a friend to this person but not a girlfriend. Until he breaks free of this addiction and separates his fantasy world from reality, he will have a warped view of women, sex, and love. Nothing will ever measure up in his mind to what he has been exposed to through porn. Run fast and far from this type of guy. I know this sounds extreme, but if you saw the devastation this character flaw leaves in the years to come, you would understand. I have girlfriends who are raising their kids all by themselves because their Christian husbands were leading secret double lives in chat rooms and with other women because of porn. Many of these men began their porn habits in high school. They need our prayers. Satan has used porn to entice many men, young and old, to forfeit the abundant life Christ referred to in John 10:10. Don't let him rob you of the abundant life by becoming involved in a relationship with this type of guy—steer clear! ✳

Are you the type who attracts boy friends but not boyfriends? Do you dread Valentine's Day each year? Do you wonder if you are invisible to guys? Does it bother you? I hope not. In a culture that brainwashes girls that guys should be the center of their lives, many girls feel like they are big nothings unless they have a boyfriend. At the risk of sounding like your mother, I know you may not prefer to be boyfriend-less but trust me when I say you may have the advantage in the end. Boyfriends take energy, time, and emotions. You've probably witnessed some of the fallout that can come with having a boyfriend just by watching some of your friends who have been involved in dating relationships. There are many girls (I was one) who will someday look back and wish they had remained single longer.

Rather than sit around and stew about it, use this time efficiently. The next time you are feeling frustrated over not having a boyfriend, try focusing on the following:

BOYFRIEND-LESS

You have more time to work on your relationship with your one true prince, Jesus Christ.

Use the time to focus on your own interests and preferences. Too often girls who date early conform themselves to the guy they are with and lose sight of who God intended them to be.

Concentrate on building friendships with guys. There is such freedom in being able to have boy friends rather than boyfriends and avoid all the trappings that come with a relationship.

Learn to pour out your heart before God. Boyfriend or not, this is a lifelong discipline that should be cultivated by every Christian.

If most of your good girlfriends have boyfriends and you find yourself home alone on the weekends, find some new friends!

Thank the Lord that you are spared from many of the temptations that come with having a boyfriend.

Remember that you are not alone. Sometimes it might seem like you are the only girl in the school without a boyfriend, but the truth is, you're in the majority.

If you are stressed over whether or not anyone will ask you to Homecoming or Prom, give the matter over to God. Tell him exactly how you feel. If no one ends up asking you, consider taking a guy friend or going with a group of girls.

One verse that every teen girl should memorize is Song of Songs 8:4 which says: "Young women of Jerusalem, I charge you: do not stir up or awaken love until the appropriate time."

There is absolutely no hurry in dating. When the time is right, you will know it. Do not awaken love before its time. ✳

ALL ABOUT GUYS

Prince Charming or

Discover who you REALLY want to impress . . .

You can't wait to go to the mall to:

a) run into that cute guy at the sunglasses kiosk.

b) spend quality time with your girlfriends.

When you run into the most popular guys in school, you:

a) flirt and let them know you are definitely available for a date.

b) politely say, "Hi" and be yourself.

ALL ABOUT GUYS

During school you head for the bathroom:

a) between every class to see if your hair and makeup are still perfect.

b) only when your eight glasses of water kicks in.

After school you leave your best friend a short note to tell her:

a) your secret crush just brokeup with his girlfriend and now's your chance.

b) you are so glad you're friends and what a blessing she is to you.

Your Sunday school class divides into small groups and you:

a) figure out how you can be paired up with at least one cute guy.

b) are so excited you get to share what God's been doing in your life this week.

The captain of the basketball team (and one of the hottest guys in school) is having a party while his parents are out of town (without their knowledge of course) and invites you, so:

a) you eagerly accept and plan your escape route out of the house after curfew.

You're spending some quiet time by yourself under the stars, and you:

a) can't stop thinking about how you wish you had a boyfriend.

b) can't stop thanking God for his amazing creation.

Prince of Peace?

b) you decline and tell him you already have plans (even though they involve watching LuLu, your pet fish, swim in circles).

You gauge your popularity by:

a) the number of cute guys that have you on their buddy list.

b) the number of quality friendships you have.

When you're walking the track during PE class, you are:

a) trying to catch every cute guy's attention.

b) enjoying quality time with your girlfriend and ignoring the ridiculous flirting going on all around you.

It's Sunday night youth group meeting, and you :

a) can't stop thinking about your crush on the guy playing the guitar on stage.

b) wish you felt this close to God all week

If you chose mostly (a): Hang on tight—you're in for a bumpy ride! If you have to flirt to catch a guy's attention, then you can bet that another girl will come along and steal it right back. Learn to trust God with your future. He is faithful to bring the right person along at the right time. He is much more powerful than any scheme we could come up with to get a guy!

If you chose mostly (b): You've found the right prince! You're on track to having a very peaceful life. By focusing your attention on others, you don't have to worry about all the heartache and pain that comes with superficial relationships. *

Source: Provided by Julie Shannan

25 guys tell all

We polled Christian teen guys around the country between the ages of fourteen and eighteen, and asked them this question: "If you could give girls one piece of honest advice, what would it be?" Here's what some of them said:

One thing girls should know is that it is not necessary that you have a boyfriend. I know some girls who always seem to have a boyfriend, and when they breakup with him they immediately go out and get a new one. Not only does this hurt the guy (even though you may not realize it), it hurts you. A lot of guys may act tough and nonchalant when you break up with us, but it does hurt us.
—Jeremy, 15

I would tell girls that if they knew how guys' and men's minds work, they would be more careful about what they wear—like the halter tops and shirts showing your belly. And for us good guys out there, it just makes it more difficult for us to control our natural desires. When you see your girlfriend or a married woman dressed that way, you have to wonder why she's interested in getting another guy's attention.
—Corey, 18

Some girls need to put more clothes on. It just annoys me. I also hate when they gossip. I can't stand it. —Jacob, 14

Don't curse. When a girl curses it has got to be the most unattractive thing ever. —Jared, 15

Some girls should take it easy on the makeup; there is such a thing as too much. —Wes, 18

ALL ABOUT GUYS

The greatest proof of the existence of God is a transformed life. This shows itself in whether or not a girl dresses modestly, treats others with kindness, loves with the love of God, respects authority, etc. Don't find your identity in any guy, or any person, but in God.   —Kevin, 18

Just be yourself. You shouldn't be worried what others think of you. It only matters what God thinks of you. And don't call guys or instant message them all the time; let us do that.
—Joey, 14

I personally would tell girls to be more modest, stop the cursing, and remember their morals.   —Caleb, 15

It kind of annoys me when a girl spends $200 on one outfit at the mall or does her makeup for an hour every day. I think girls should just relax more and care less about what other people think.   —Sam, 14

The one thing I would tell girls is to simply be yourself. Guys will like you for who you are, not by how you dress or who you hang out with. Be comfortable with who you are, and don't change what you say or how you feel because you're afraid of how others will perceive you or if they will accept you. Be honest and don't be afraid to be how God made you to be.   —John, 15

Don't wear so much makeup! I think it makes girls come off as materialistic or fake. Also, I think girls should be happy with the bodies God gave them and not try to change what is already perfect. Don't change for any guy because if a guy likes you then he should like you for you, not for the way you dress or the way you look.   —Preston, 18

If there was one piece of advice that I would give to girls, it is that they shouldn't do so much with guys. Honestly, to me it is a total turn off if I know that a girl has been around. Besides it doesn't make you look cool—it just makes you look like you are desperate.
—Jordon, 15

My advice to girls deals with self-esteem in dating relationships. I think that it's important for women to understand fully that they are beautiful creations that God has made, and they should be treated accordingly in a relationship. I think that too often girls settle for guys that treat them poorly instead of waiting for the knight in shining armor they have always dreamed of. Ladies, wait for your knight; he's coming.
—Jake, 18

Just be yourself. Don't try to be who or what you think a guy wants you to be. After all, what drew my attention was seeing you be who you are in school or church or wherever we met. I am drawn to girls who speak intelligently, don't gossip (I need to feel sure you won't share things about us to others.), like to have fun, smile, and are not afraid to disagree with me.   —Aaron, 18

I wish girls would realize that a sincere love of Christ makes them beautiful in the most lovable way.   —Matt, 18

If I could give girls one piece of advice, it would be simply to dress modestly and please do not wear tight shirts that show your stomach. Not only will seeing a little bulge of skin and fat hanging out keep guys away; it's just plain disgusting. Seriously, who wants to see that? Just wear clothes that allow a guy to keep his mind and attention focused on the amazing girl you are on the inside.   —Kyle, 17

ALL ABOUT GUYS

Many girls want to feel wanted and worth something, so they dress to get attention. For some odd reason they think showing off their body might create a desire within us guys to like them for who they are, but instead it makes us guys more interested in the girl's body than the girl. If girls are searching for someone they can put their trust, hope, and feelings in, then they should rely on God and become stable in him before searching for a significant other. Dress modestly so the qualities you want guys to see within you will grab their attention.   —Ben, 18

Some advice I would give girls is not to lay on the makeup. Too much makeup makes me think that's all that person thinks about. Also, don't wear the really revealing clothes because some guys will just stare instead of looking you in the eyes. Sure, some guys will look but not for the right reasons.   —Michael, 15

My advice to girls is: I don't think it's necessary for girls to cake on makeup just to look like they have a perfect face. Sure, a little makeup is OK, but the natural look is definitely more attractive than looking like a clown. Show your natural beauty; show what God gave you.   — Alex, 16

I would want girls to know that sex may seem like "the answer" to most teens, but someday, when Christian guys are looking for someone to marry, they will want a pure girl.   —Tyler, 14

Remember that every single guy, no matter how noble or how pure he is, still struggles with temptation. The nicest guys who long for and desire purity still need your help, even when it seems like we're strong. Satan grabs a hold of us and makes us want things that we shouldn't want and we shouldn't have, and the best thing you could do for us is also to be strong and tell us when we're out of line.   —Jeremy, 18

I would tell girls that dressing immodestly isn't the way to attract Christian guys. For me and the vast majority of Christian guys I know, showing too much skin is a turnoff. If you want to impress a guy, I would suggest a nice pair of jeans and a T-shirt. We'd prefer that to a halter top and a miniskirt any day.   —Oliver, 15

Don't be desperate for guys to like you. If you are always calling, IM-ing, and coming over, it gets annoying after awhile. Relax and be yourself. Let us chase after you for once.   —Ryan, 16

Girls who smoke are really unattractive. And if you dress in a revealing way, then that's how people look at you, like you're a girl who will show them everything and will do just about anything with guys.   —Colby, 16

Don't sell out who you are in order to become what you think a guy wants. If you are godly, you will attract a godly guy.

—Matt, 18 *

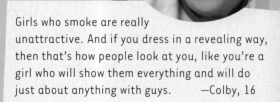

ALL ABOUT GUYS

the
Scoop
on
S·E·X

what's your plan?

"It happened so fast I didn't have time to think." If I had a nickel for every high school or college girl who has said that to me at a conference, I'd be a rich woman. In every situation they found themselves in that uncomfortable position of being alone with a guy they liked, and before they knew it, things had gotten out of hand. If only they had a plan! Isaiah 32:8 says, "But a noble person plans noble things; he stands up for noble causes."

So what about you? Do you have a plan? Do you know what to say when faced with sexual temptation? Most girls fall into sexual sin because they don't have a plan. I will tell you exactly what I tell other girls about coming up with a plan. I tell them to start by first going before God and determining how far is too far. A good rule of thumb is to draw the line at anything that would make you feel uncomfortable if Jesus were present (and rest assured he is!). I am not going to launch into a sermon about whether or not it's OK to kiss because some couples can successfully stop at kissing. Others cannot. Only you know if you can. If you can but your boyfriend can't, you have your answer.

Next I tell girls how important it is to be able to put into words what their limit or plan is. Many girls are caught off guard and have no clue what to say in the heat of the moment. Most end up compromising their purity. If you are committed to sexual purity, but afraid you might get tongue-tied in a tempting situation, **try practicing a few of these one-liners in front of your mirror, or better yet, come up with something on your own:**

"You need to stop. I'm not comfortable with this."

"Whoa . . . we need to talk about this."

"Sorry, but my limit is _____ (holding hands, kissing). Everything else I'm saving for marriage."

If your date is a real jerk and continues to persist, try these . . .

"Whoa, dude! Have you had your hearing checked lately? Take me home now."

"Hang on, let me check in with my dad and make sure he's OK with this."

"Wow. And I thought you were a nice guy. Time to take me home."

Here's the bottom line: **Girls who go into their teen years with a plan and the determination to stick to their plan are less likely to go too far sexually.** It's as simple as that. If you go out with a guy, you don't owe him anything. And remember: Any guy who refuses to respect your limits is not a guy you want to spend time with. You mean way too much to God to sacrifice your purity for some guy who just wants a momentary thrill. Don't flatter yourself by thinking that a guy's sexual persistence proves you are desirable. His persistence may mean that he has perceived you as an easy target. Guys sense up front which girls won't and which girls will. What sort of message are you sending? Come up with a plan before it's too late. Practice your plan, stick to your plan, and ask a friend to hold you accountable to your plan. It's not a matter of "if" you will need a plan, it's a matter when. ✳

Guys sense up front which girls won't and which girls will.

BEWARE OF THE HOOK-UP TREND

I had a roommate in college who was the chaplain of her sorority. She was in charge of opening the meetings in prayer and organizing small-group Bible studies. When her birthday rolled around, I set out in search of a Christian tape (no such thing as CDs yet!) that she had told me she wanted earlier in the month. I was not a Christian at the time, and I recall the awkwardness of walking into a Christian bookstore. Maria's faith was a mystery to me. I was searching for meaning and purpose in my life but resistant to embrace Christianity based on some unfortunate episodes of hypocrisy I had witnessed in my earlier years. I was watching Maria closely to see if she was any different from some of the Christians I had known in the past who couldn't seem to match their walk with their talk. Unfortunately, I wouldn't have to watch long. Maria and I were talking about a date she had been on the night before with a guy she had met at a mixer (a party where a sorority and a fraternity get together). She had been really excited about this date so I couldn't wait to hear about the details.

Unfortunately, she gave me way more details than I ever wanted to know. She told me that it was very clear by the end of the date that he wanted "something." She shrugged it off and said, "So I gave him what he wanted so he would leave me alone—we didn't have sex but, you know . . ." I was shocked. I would never do such a thing, and yet she was the Christian!

In my day, behavior like that was considered unacceptable. In fact, we had a name for girls who "hooked up" with guys for one-night stands. Unfortunately, what my roommate did is common in teen culture today. Girls and guys "hook up" to mess around sexually. Some go all the way, and others come close. Many who have been brainwashed by television, movies, music, and fashion magazines shrug it off as no big deal. There was even a study done among college women that determined dating has pretty much been replaced by "hooking up." Girls interviewed in the study claimed that guys have come to expect hook ups. Many girls expressed frustration that very few guys will go to the trouble to work up their nerve to ask a girl out on a formal date, pay for the date, and behave as a perfect gentleman by expecting nothing in return at the end of the date, especially when so many girls are willing to hook up for free, no strings attached. The study also revealed that **hook ups were taking an emotional toll on the girls.** In light of the culture's cry for sexual freedom and the right to have sex and/or mess around with no obligations, girls couldn't seem to rationalize it away like the guys.

God created sex to be a beautiful expression of love between a husband and a wife. **When sex or sexual activity is practiced outside of marriage, it will always lead to emptiness and confusion.** Shame may not follow immediately, but rest assured, it will follow. Girls are not wired to hook up casually with guys without suffering emotional consequences. Many girls will hook up as a means to get the attention they desperately crave from guys.

Shame may not follow immediately, but rest assured, it will follow.

Christian girls know better than to settle for this kind of negative attention. For one, it is sin, and sin will never fill the void in your heart. Secondly, **you are a child of the king and set apart for great things—not casual one-night stands.** Your worth should come from knowing you are loved beyond measure by the God of this universe. Make it a habit to bask in the glow of his perfect love. You deserve respect, but first you must respect yourself. ✳

BIG 5 LIES ABOUT SEX

There are a lot of lies floating around out there when it comes to sex—especially in high school. Below, you will find five common lies that you will probably hear before you graduate from high school along with the truth you need to know to keep you from believing them.

with the mainstream media and their routine use of sex to boost ratings and peddle product." The article further acknowledges that religion plays a critical role, as well as caring parents, a sense of the teen's own unreadiness, and a desire to gain control over their destinies.[2]

> It would be easy to assume that everyone is having sex based on the attention it gets in media ads, music, television, and magazines.

LIE 1: EVERYONE IS DOING IT.

It would be easy for girls to assume that everyone is having sex based on the attention it gets in media ads, movies, music, television, and magazines. The truth is that a majority of high school students are not doing it. In fact, survey results indicate that sexual activity among high school students is actually declining. In 2001, 45.6 percent of high school students reported they had had sex. Compare that to 54 percent in 1991.[1] A December 2002 cover story in *Newsweek* read: "The New Virginity: Why More Teens are Choosing Not to Have Sex." The article says this "wave of young adults represents a new counterculture, one clearly at odds

LIE 2: AS LONG AS YOU LOVE THE PERSON, IT'S OK TO HAVE SEX.

In a culture where the lines of morality have been blurred, many teens have justified that sex is acceptable as long as you love the person. This lie assumes that teens have a proper understanding of what constitutes "true love." So what is true love? True love says, "I love and respect you enough to wait until we are married." In 1 Corinthians 13, *love* is defined as not being "self-seeking."

True love is demonstrated when two people respect each other enough to resist the temptations to have pre-marital sex based on their concern for each other's well-being. I cannot imagine a girl out there that doesn't desire to be loved and respected in that way. In a culture that is focused on self and looking out for #1, it is rare to find displays of the type of true love spoken of in 1 Corinthians 13. Do you really want to marry a guy who has slept around with a lot of different girls? I didn't think so. If anything, it's a sign that he can't resist temptation and he gives in easily to sin. The same goes for you. When it comes to marriage, guys don't like used goods. That may sound harsh, but it's true.

> True love is demonstrated when two people respect each other enough to resist the temptations to have premarital sex based on their concern for each other's well-being.

While this new virginity wave is encouraging, keep in mind that a majority of high school seniors have had sex by graduation, and an overwhelming majority will have sex before marriage, so we still have a long way to go.

And what about those virginity pledges? According to a federal survey, 9 percent of boys and 16 percent of girls in middle and high schools say they've taken a virginity pledge.[3] Unfortunately, it was also found that while virginity pledges were effective at postponing sex, the promise often wore off after an average of eighteen months, and many of the teens who signed the pledge ended up having sex before marriage. Overall, purity pledges are good, but teens need to remember that the promise they made to God was to save sex until marriage rather than just postpone it for a year or so.

Also, if he (or you) has given into sex before marriage, what's to keep him (or you) from giving into sex with someone else after marriage? Think about it.

LIE 3: IT'S NOT SEX UNLESS YOU GO ALL THE WAY.

As unpleasant as this topic is to discuss, it is necessary given the times. Oral sex among teens is on the increase, especially among the younger teens. Surveys show that oral sex is viewed by many teens as no big deal. One Arlington, Virginia, middle schooler explained, "It's a sexual thing that keeps us from having sex."[4] An article in *USA Today* reported abstinence programs do not give a

comprehensive approach to what teens should "abstain" from and commonly focus only on abstaining from the act of sexual intercourse. One fifteen-year-old girl stated in the article, "The consensus in my high school is that oral sex makes girls popular, whereas intercourse would make them outcasts."[5]

In my years of ministry to teen girls, I have heard heart-breaking stories concerning this epidemic of oral sex among teens. One story involved a fourteen-year-old captain of the cheerleading squad who performed oral sex on a boy in a hot tub at a party while her classmates stood by and watched. Do you realize the shame this girl will carry for the rest of her life? Don't be fooled—that kind of thing lives with you for-ever. And don't think for a minute that this kind of stuff is not going on with "Christian" teens. I am blown away by the number of stories I hear that involve church kids partici-pating in this kind of behavior. They should know better!

Physician and radio host Drew Pinsky has a Web site where many teens go to talk about sex. He is hearing from many young teens that engage in oral sex and consider it as "just a part of making out." Pinsky also thinks the act is often degrading to young girls. "Their perception is that it's

> Sex is only 100 percent safe when an individual abstains from sex until marriage and marries someone who has done the same.

empowering. Really it is the exact opposite. The message they get is this is how to get and keep a man."[6]

I wish teen girls could see the shame and remorse so many adult women carry over sexual promiscuity in their teen years. We are wired to know when something is wrong so it is no surprise that many who have sex (oral and/or inter-course) outside of marriage end up carrying guilt and shame over their actions in the years that follow. Of course, we know that God will forgive and forget our sins, but unfor-tunately we don't have the same luxury of forgetting them. If you have already messed up in this area, be sure to read "What if I've Already Blown It?" on pages 120–121. Fortunately, with God it is never too late to begin again.

LIE 4: CONDOMS PROTECT AGAINST UNWANTED PREG-NANCIES AND SEXUALLY TRANSMITTED DISEASES [STDS].

Perhaps, one of the greatest tragedies taught in sex education classes is that there is such a thing as "safe sex." **Sex is only 100 percent safe when an individual abstains from sex until marriage and marries someone who has also done the same.** Often, the "safe sex" statistics regarding the ability of condoms to protect against unwanted preg-nancies and STDs make the unrealistic assumption that condoms will be used 100 percent of the time with a zero percent failure rate. Even 100 percent condom use does not eliminate the risk of any STD, including HIV.[7]

Further, teens need to be told that even when condoms are used every time, they can at best only provide a 50 per-cent reduction in the transmission rates of Syphilis, Gonorrhea, and Chlamydia. Condoms do not appear to pro-vide any protection from HPV, which causes 99 percent of all cervical cancer. Clearly, as the Medical Institute for Sexual

Health has determined, "safer sex isn't nearly safe enough."[8]

When I was a freshman in college, I was asked out by an incredibly handsome, funny, and charming guy. He was the kind of guy that could pretty much get any girl he wanted, and many of my friends had confessed to liking him. So when he asked me out, I felt like the lucky one. A few weeks after we went out, a friend told me that he had herpes and had given it to his ex-girlfriend! Fortunately, I was not the promiscuous type who slept around with guys, or I could have contracted an incurable disease. I never went out with him again and this handsome, funny, and charming guy quickly became undesirable to the girls on campus once the news spread. His reputation was ruined, and he carried the stigma of having an STD. His ex-girlfriend went on to marry someone else after college, and my friend who knew her later told me that she suffered long and hard over the stress of having to tell the man she was going to marry that she was infected with an incurable disease. **She was fortunate that he married her anyway. She will forever carry this painful reminder of having sex outside of marriage.** Her husband will be forced to wear a condom to protect himself from contracting the disease. She will have to deliver her babies by C-section to prevent them from passing through the birth canal and contracting the disease. She will also suffer painful flair-ups from the disease forever. Big price to pay for a few moments of pleasure, if you ask me.

sex throughout the ages without having to experiment by sleeping around before marriage? I have yet to meet one single married couple who "couldn't figure out what to do!" Trust me on this one—you will know what to do.

If you have reasoned that sex outside of marriage will make you more experienced on your wedding night, remember this: Any physical pleasure you may gain on your wedding night from "experience," will be lessened by the fact that you gained that experience from sex with someone else, outside of marriage, and outside of the will of God. **Why not follow God's plan and wait until your wedding night and enjoy sex without any regrets?** Remember, God created sex to be an emotional, physical, and spiritual experience between a husband and wife in marriage. **Don't settle for less.** If you are still tempted in this area, be sure to check out "A Tale of Three Brides" on pages 125–126.

Any physical pleasure you may gain on your wedding night from "experience," will be lessened by the fact that you gained that experience from sex with someone else, outside of marriage, and outside of the will of God.

LIE 5: IF YOU DON'T HAVE SEX, YOU WON'T KNOW WHAT TO DO WHEN YOU'RE MARRIED.

This is perhaps the most ridiculous lie of all. Give me a break! Here are some facts to consider:

The first time is always awkward, so would you rather experience that brief awkwardness with someone you won't likely marry or with someone who loves you enough to give you a ring, say "I do," and commit to spend the rest of his life with you?

As for those who fear they will "not know what to do on their wedding night," oh, please! Do you realize how ridiculous that statement is considering people have been having

So, there you have it. The top five lies about sex and the real truth. Don't keep this great scoop to yourself—friends tell friends the truth. ✳

---

1. http://www.cdc.gov/mmwr/preview/mmwrhtml/ss5104a1.htm#fig7; YRBS, 2001; Center for Disease Control.
2. *Newsweek*, 9 December 2992, 61.
3. Neil Howe and William Strauss, *Millenials Rising: The Next Great Generation* (New York: Vintage Books, 2000), 200.
4. Ibid., 201.
5. "Sex/Not Sex: For Many Teens, Oral Doesn't Count," *USA Today*, 16 November 2000, front page cover story.
6. Ibid.
7. "Sex, Condoms, and STDs: What We Now Know," *The Medical Institute for Sexual Health*, Austin, Texas, 2002.
8. Ibid.

top five

reasons to save sex until you are married

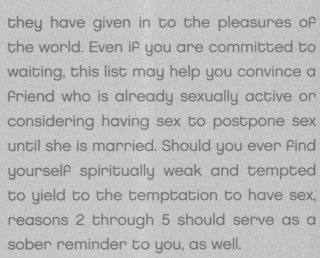

If you're a Christian, chances are good that the "don't have sex until you are married" speech is ringing in your ears. Yet sometimes parents and youth ministers are so busy telling you to say "I don't" until you say "I do" that we fail to remind you of the why behind the message.

Below are five reasons to remind you why you should wait, until you are married to have sex. The first reason alone is reason enough to wait and no other reasons are even necessary. However, there are some Christian girls, who for whatever reason, choose to ignore God's rules regarding sex. They have been taught that sex outside of marriage is wrong, but they have given in to the pleasures of the world. Even if you are committed to waiting, this list may help you convince a friend who is already sexually active or considering having sex to postpone sex until she is married. Should you ever find yourself spiritually weak and tempted to yield to the temptation to have sex, reasons 2 through 5 should serve as a sober reminder to you, as well.

top five reasons

1. Your body is not your own; it belongs to God.

First Corinthians 6:18–20 should be memorized by every preteen and teen before they encounter sexual temptation. It reads:

"Flee from sexual immorality! 'Every sin a person can commit is outside the body,' but the person who is sexually immoral sins against his own body. Do you not know that your body is a sanctuary of the Holy Spirit who is in you, whom you have from God? You are not your own, for you were bought at a price; therefore glorify God in your body."

Virginity pledges that are made to God cover not only sexual intercourse but other sexually impure acts, as well. I am disturbed by the number Christian teens that have justified that "everything but sexual intercourse is OK."

2. A large majority of teen girls who have sex regret it.

Seventy-two percent of teen girls regret their decision to have sex and wish they had waited.[1] While our culture has brainwashed young women into thinking that empowerment includes the right to have sex with no strings attached, true empowerment is found in saying no to sex before marriage. Additionally, 89 percent of teen girls surveyed in a 2002 study said their peers (teen girls) feel pressure from boys to have sex.[2]

It is not uncommon for girls who have had sex to attempt to convince their friends to have sex. Even though most girls regret the decision, it makes them feel they are not alone in their decision if most everyone they know is doing it. The saying rings true, "misery loves company." It makes no sense to have sex outside of marriage if a majority of girls regret it. Out of the girls who choose to wait until marriage to have sex, zero pecent end up having regrets. The choice is simple. Do you want to be in the category where 72 percent have regrets or zero percent have regrets?

3. High likelihood of a bad reputation.

Ninety-one percent of teens surveyed said a girl can get a bad reputation if she has sex.[3] Girls may think that the boys will like them more if they have sex, but in reality boys respect the girls who choose to save sex for marriage. In the same survey, 92 percent of teens said it is generally considered a good thing for a girl to be a virgin.[4] Remember that the next time anyone implies that it's uncool to be a virgin.

One teen boy confirms the above: "Dear Abby: I'm a guy, eighteen, and I have something to say to girls who sleep around. They may think they are 'hot stuff,' but they should hear what is said about them in the locker room. These poor girls think it is flattering to be sought out—that it is a compliment to have sex. Not so! It is cheap and degrading to be used."[5] Ouch, the truth hurts.

4. One in four will get a sexually transmitted disease (STD).

One out of four sexually active teens gets a sexually transmitted disease every year.[6] Let me put that in perspective for you: If you were to line up one hundred teens who are sexually active, a whopping twenty-five of them would be infected with a STD. What that means for the girl who is promiscuous and sleeps around, if she has sex with four guys, chances are good that at least one would have a STD. Some STDs are incurable, and others can hinder or even prevent young women from bearing children. Try to imagine the embarrassment of having to explain to your future husband that you have a STD. If you save sex until marriage, you don't have to worry about getting a STD or experiencing the embarrassment of having to explain your STD to your husband.

5. Forty percent will become pregnant.

If none of the above reasons is enough to sway a girl from having sex before marriage, perhaps the reality of this one will. A whopping 40 percent of teen girls will become pregnant at least once by the age of twenty.[7] Therefore, four of every ten teen girls will be faced with the reality of raising a child, placing a child up for adoption, or having an abortion. Regardless of which choice is made, emotional scars will leave their mark for years to come. One third of all babies born in this country are born to unwed mothers.[8] Each day, approximately eleven hundred teen girls will have an abortion. If you do the math, that's nearly half a million babies a year whose lives are snuffed out by teens who are unwilling to suffer the consequences for their actions. Those who are noble enough to give their babies up for adoption will suffer emotional scars of a different sort for years to come. Is sex outside of marriage really worth the risk?

If God says to wait, we need to wait.

So, now you have the facts. Again, no other reason is needed other than reason number 1. If God says to wait, we need to wait. For the person who is in spiritual rebellion, reasons 2 through 5 leave them with little excuse. Having sex outside of marriage doesn't add up. *

1. *Seventeen*, January 2003, 114.
2. Ibid.
3. Ibid.
4. Ibid.
5. *Austin American Statesman*, no date.
6. *Seventeen*, January 2003, 115.
7. National Campaign to Prevent Teen Pregnancy, 2002.
8. Census 2000, FOF Report.

what if i've already blown it?

I remember my first big lesson in the value of patience. Christmas was one week away, and under the tree was a beautifully wrapped present with my name on it. My mom built the anticipation by commenting on it daily. "It's nothing you've ever mentioned wanting, but I hope you like it." She explained that it was my main present due to the cost. *What in the world could it be?* I wondered. Finally, I couldn't take it any longer. The suspense was killing me.

My parents were at work, and I was home alone. I took the gift and carefully unwrapped one end. I slipped the box neatly out of the paper. I opened the box lid and pulled back the tissue paper. Inside the box I found a book (for the purpose of weighting the gift down) and a small velvet jewelry box. I slowly opened the lid to the jewelry box and found a beautiful diamond and gold ring. I put the ring on my finger and it fit perfectly. After sufficiently admiring it on my hand, I put the ring back in its box and carefully rewrapped the present. I placed it in the exact spot under the tree. No wonder my mom was excited about giving me this gift! Instantly I was filled with regret. The gift was meant to be opened Christmas, but my impatience had gotten the best of me. It wouldn't be the same when I unwrapped it again on Christmas morning. Oh, how I wish I had waited. If only I could go back and do it all over again.

Unfortunately, I failed to learn my lesson with the ring and suffered a much greater loss a year later. I opened another gift early. This gift was from God and was meant for my wedding night. If only I could go back and do it all over again.[1]

I know many girls can relate to the regret I felt over losing my virginity to someone who was not my husband. **If you are one of them, it's never too late to commit to purity.** In fact, I am a living testimony of someone who blew it but later made a pledge to wait until my wedding night. Although I cannot technically say I was a virgin when I married, I can proudly say that my husband and I waited.

> **If you are in a relationship where you are sexually active, it is never too late to do the right thing.**

If you are in a relationship where you are sexually active, it is never too late to do the right thing. Be warned that it is near impossible to return to the sweet and innocent phase with the same guy once you have given in physically. **True commitment may require a breakup. While this may be a painful thought, remember that any guy who pressures you sexually after you've set clear boundaries, isn't a guy worth having. Period.**

I know it's hard for teenagers to think past the moment, but try to think ahead and imagine the pride you will feel on your wedding night. Even though I blew it, I still had great pride that I waited with my husband until our wedding night. **By waiting, we grew to trust and respect each other in other areas.** Make the "I do" more special by saying "I don't" before you are married. ✳

1. Vicki Courtney, *Your Girl* (Nashville, Tenn.: Broadman & Holman Publishers, 2004), 85–86.

What Do You Think of Me?

From baby steps and finger paints
and learning how to read,
I proudly asked the world's advice,
"What do you think of me?"

With trophies, grades and honors
I quickly began to see
the world applauds success and fame—
"What do you think of me?"

"You look great," "You smell good,"
"You've lost some weight, I see."
With high school comes the dating game—
"What do you think of me?"

For boyfriends and promised love,
I traded my purity,
and choked back tears and silently asked,
"What do you think of me?"

The world's applause was my reward
when I sought to please,
but the clapping stopped when I missed the mark—
"What do you think of me?"

And now I stand before His throne
burdened by sin and shame.
Beaten and battered by the world,
I call upon His name.

I hold back tears and try to speak,
but utter a silent plea.
With downcast eyes, I finally ask,
"What do you think of me?"

I catch my breath as He draws close
In fear, my knees grow weak.
My heart grows faint as I wait on Him
And then I hear Him speak:

"My child," He said, "the time has come
when you ask the same of Me.
For so long you've sought the world's advice—
What do you think of me?"

"Now here we are, My turn has come,
the chance to finally say
exactly what I think of you,
so allow Me, if I may."

Gently, He takes my chin
and raises my face to see.
"My child," He said, "You're beautiful—
you're made in the image of Me!"

"The world was quick to judge your deeds,
but failed to tell the rest—
there was nothing you could do
to make Me love you less."

"Before you ever drew a breath,
My name was on your heart,
the Author of your hidden frame
before your life did start."

"You entered this life with pomp and fare
And I held my breath to see,
if those I allowed to care for you
would teach you all about Me."

"An innocent child, your journey began
in this life to find your place.
The world was quick to take your hand
and thus began the race."

"In quiet moments throughout your life
I whispered in your ear,
tender pledges of My love—
I hoped someday you'd hear."

"But the world could offer nothing
to fill your inmost need,
and release you from the bondage of sin
and love you eternally."

"My Son was sent to tell the world
of My unfailing love.
A covenant pledged to all mankind
and written in heaven above."

"My boy was nailed to a rugged cross,
For you, He agreed to die.
Burdened by your sin and shame,
'It is finished,' He finally cried."

"The world could never match My love,
the price was far too high—
for if you were the only one,
My Son would choose to die."

"I've gone to desperate lengths, My child,
to prove My love to you.
I loved you then, I love you now—
Will you love Me too?"

"My child," He said,"The choice is yours.
What will your answer be?
It's your turn now—the question is,
What do you think of Me?"

—Vicki Courtney ©1999

A Tale of Three Brides

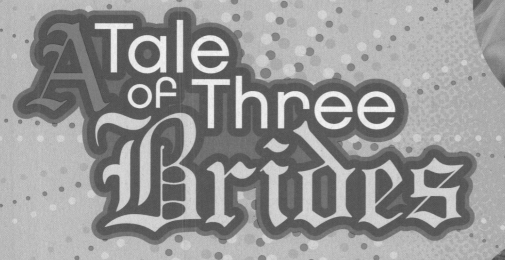

Once upon a time, there were three brides.

Each bride had been given a large, beautifully wrapped gift with a silver ribbon when they were just little girls. Each gift came with the same tag that read:

Precious Daughter,
Do not open until your wedding night. This gift is meant to be shared with your husband.

Love, God

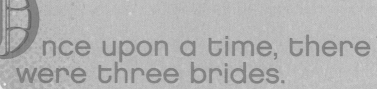

Well, I wish I could tell you that all three brides heeded the instructions. One bride opened her gift long before she met her husband. In fact, she shared "the gift" over and over again, sometimes with guys she hardly even knew! When it came time for her wedding night, she didn't even bother to take the gift with her. **What did it matter anyway? she thought. It had ceased to be a gift the day she opened it.** Besides, she had seen the unwrapped box in the back of her closet not long ago, and it was tattered and worn. Certainly, not something fit to take on your wedding night.

But to her shock, her husband brought his gift along and presented it on their wedding night. It looked much like that gift tossed in the back of her closet. She explained that she didn't bother to bring her gift because it was so old and secondhand. Regardless, they agreed to open his gift as the instructions had said on the box, even though they had not waited. The beautiful wrapping had long since been ripped off, and the bow was gone. The box was bent, torn, and falling apart. When they removed the lid and peered inside, they were confused. **The bride spoke first and said, "I don't get it—what's so special about this gift?"** Then they both sat there in silence. The bride wondered to herself why the box was so used. *Has he taken the gift and shared it with others?* she wondered. The thought was certainly unsettling, but the thought that followed sent a chill up her spine. What would keep him from sharing the gift with others in the future if he had already done so in the past? Didn't this gift belong exclusively to her, now?

At the same time her husband was deep in thought, wondering why she had left her gift behind and shrugged it off so easily. I mean, sure, we may not have followed the directions on our gifts, but couldn't it still be special? And then he wondered how many men she had shared the gift with over the years—the gift that was meant to be his exclusively. The thought certainly left him feeling insecure about the future. His thoughts continued. *Why did we build up so much excitement over the wedding and honeymoon in the first place? I mean, we've already shared a bed and many of the things that married people share. What's so special about a wedding and a honeymoon?* And then they both found themselves thinking, *Maybe this is the very reason we were supposed to wait to open the gift.* But it was too late.

The second bride also unwrapped her gift early, but she experienced great regret. So she made a vow to take better care of the gift and save it for her wedding night, just as the directions said. When it came time for her wedding night, she presented the gift to her husband, and he presented his to her. His gift was brand-new, and she felt a pang of conviction that she could not offer him the same in return. Even though she regretted her mistake, she was grateful that her gift had never been shared with her husband until this moment. While it would not be as special as God intended, it was still special.

The third bride had heeded the instructions that came with her gift. She treated it with loving care knowing that it was a gift from God. Her husband had also saved his gift for the wedding night, though at times he had been tempted to open the gift early. On their wedding night they had no regrets. Each one felt respected and honored that so great a gift had been saved for the other. After their wedding night, they felt secure in their relationship knowing that if someone can trust God and believe him at his word, they will likely do so in the future. And with that thought, they both felt great pity for their many friends who had opened their gifts early.

What about you? Which bride will you be? ✳

> On their wedding night, they had no regrets. Each one felt respected and honored that so great a gift had been saved for the other.

HOLLYWOOD JES

IN Mark 8:27, Jesus asked his disciples, "Who do people say that I am?" They answered him, "John the Baptist; others, Elijah; still others, one of the prophets." You can hardly blame Jesus for asking. By that time he had performed plenty of miracles. He had healed Simon's mother-in-law of a fever and a man with leprosy. He had healed a paralyzed man who had been lowered through a roof by his friends. He had healed a deaf and dumb man, another man who was blind, fed five thousand people with five loaves of bread and two fish, raised a twelve-year-old child from the dead, and healed countless sick people, including a hemorrhaging woman who barely touched the cloak of his robe. He cast demons out of many people, including a man who was possessed by a "legion" of demons. It was quite a show when Jesus redirected the demons into a herd of two thousand pigs and they rushed down a steep hillside into a lake and drowned. Oh, and did I mention that he had walked on water? Any one of these events would have been front-page news in today's world. Likely word had spread from village to village of this man, Jesus and his many miracles.

Stop for a minute and imagine what sort of answers Jesus would get if he posed the same question, "Who do people say I am" to his disciples today. "Well, let's see Lord, Madonna says you are a great teacher. Ashton Kutcher sports a trendy T-shirt that boldly proclaims you are his homeboy. In the movie *Bruce Almighty* it talks a lot about God, but you didn't get a part. Ditto for the popular show, *Touched by an Angel*. You did, however, get a part in *South*

Park—as the host of a cable access show called *Jesus and Friends*. Unfortunately, they didn't always portray you in a positive light. Hollywood will occasionally take a stab at making a made-for-TV movie or a feature-length movie that depicts your life. Unfortunately, most producers fail to consult with you and end up fashioning their own custom-made Jesus. The exception is Mel Gibson—his movie would make you real proud.

When it comes to pop music, Jessica Simpson sang that you are her portion in the hymn, "His Eye Is on the Sparrow." She included the song on one of her CDs—you know, the one called "Irresistible," where she poses seductively on the front cover in a see-through blouse. Popular retailer Urban Outfitters sold you as a refrigerator magnet dressed in white briefs and hanging on the cross. The $14 "Jesus Dress-Up Kit" came complete with a variety of magnetic costumes including a hula skirt and a Satan mask. Abercrombie & Fitch mentioned you in their controversial quarterly catalog that advertised "Group Sex" on the front cover. The reference made to you in the catalog is so blasphemous, we cannot bear to repeat it in your presence. You are available on e-Bay as a dash board bobble head doll for a mere eight dollars. When it comes to people searching for information about you online, you are googled slightly more than The Beatles but sometimes less than Britney Spears. And when it comes to American teenagers, 82 percent call themselves Christians, but unfortunately 53 percent of these same teenagers claim that you committed sins while on earth.[1]

Perhaps with a tear in his eye, Jesus would reply in the same way he did to the disciples so many years ago when he said, "But what about you? Who do you say I am?" And in the end, this is the million-dollar question for each and every person. The answer will determine whether or not we spend eternity with God or apart from God, so the question must be pondered carefully. Will you answer correctly as Peter did when he said, "You are the Christ" (the Messiah, the Son of God). Scripture is clear when it says that "for this reason God also highly exalted Him and gave Him the name that is above every name, so that at the name of Jesus every knee should bow—of those who are in heaven and on earth and under the earth—and every tongue should confess that Jesus Christ is Lord, to the glory of God the Father" (Phil. 2:9–11). Regardless of who those in Hollywood and today's pop culture say Jesus is, in the end, whether in heaven or hell, every knee will bow and every tongue confess, "Jesus Christ is Lord."

Who do you say he is?

---

1. See www.barna.org/FlexPage.aspx?Page=Topic&TopicID=37).

when is "good" good enough?

how many of you have heard, "As long as you're a good person, you'll go to heaven?" I'm pretty sure I said it myself before I became a Christian. Years ago I did an informal survey at an event for middle and high school girls and asked the question, "What does it take to go to heaven?" Most of the girls at the event were Christians, so I couldn't believe it when most of the answers they turned in related to good deeds and being "good."

The bottom line is that we will never be good enough in our own merit to earn God's favor. I remember an example that a speaker used at an event years ago that really drove the point home for me. He said to imagine there were three men who claimed they could successfully jump across the Grand Canyon. One was just an average guy. The second guy was athletic. The third guy was an Olympic gold medalist in the long jump. The first guy took off running to make the jump and made it about ten feet out and plunged into the canyon. The second guy was more confident, knowing he was in good physical shape. He took off running and made it out about fourteen feet and plunged into the canyon. The third guy was not the most qualitied as an Olympic long jump champion. If there was ever a guy that could jump the Grand Canyon, this was the one. With confidence he took off running and made a record jump of thirty feet and plunged into the canyon. The average width of the Grand Canyon is ten miles, which converts to about 52,800 feet. It didn't matter how much the Olympic long-jump champion had trained or how many feet he could jump—in the end, he would come up about 52,770 feet short.

It doesn't matter how good we are because we will never be able to match the purity and goodness of God.

It is the same way when it comes to earning our way to heaven based on good deeds. Isaiah 64:6 says that, "All of us have become like something unclean, and all our righteous acts are like a polluted garment." It doesn't matter how good we are because it will never be able to match the purity and goodness of God. God cannot be in the presence of any sin, so if you have sinned even once (and trust me, you have), you cannot be in his presence. Of course that is what the good news is all about. Jesus Christ came to bridge the gap between a sinful man and a Holy God. The Bible tells us that there is no forgiveness without the shedding of blood (see Hebrews 9:22 NIV). When Jesus died on the cross, the shedding of His blood became the sacrifice for our sins. Those who believe in Jesus Christ acknowledge that he has paid the penalty for their sins and they stand righteous before God. God does not see their sins because they are washed clean by the blood of Christ.

God's righteousness through faith in Jesus Christ, to all who believe, since there is no distinction. For all have sinned and fall short of the glory of God. They are justified freely by His grace through the redemption that is in Christ Jesus. God presented Him as a propitiation through faith in His blood, to demonstrate His righteousness, because in His restraint God passed over the sins previously committed. He presented Him to demonstrate His righteousness at the present time, so that He would be righteous and declare righteous the one who has faith in Jesus (Romans 3:22–26).

While the Bible tells us to seek to please God and do good works, there is no way to do enough good works to reach God on our own. We need help to make it across the Grand Canyon of sin. It doesn't matter how "good" we are; we will always fall short. Only Jesus can help you make the jump.

Most other world religions are based on man trying to be "good enough" to earn God's favor. Christianity is a beautiful picture of a loving, Holy God who reaches down to man in his sinful state and says, "I'll take you just as you are." The amazing thing is that once the reality of that kind of unconditional love begins to sink in, you are motivated to do "good" as a result of the gratitude that you feel in your heart. God stands on the other side of the Grand Canyon waiting. Don't make the jump without Jesus.

GOD IS NOT A VENDING MACHINE!

I remember lying in bed at night when I was a little girl and making my first attempts to talk to God. Even though I was not raised going to church, my mom was faithful to model prayer for me at a young age. Sometimes she would pray a common prayer rhyme with me at bedtime that I still remember today. It goes like this:

"Now I lay me down to sleep. I pray the Lord my soul to keep. If I should die before I wake, I pray the Lord my soul to take."

If you ask me, that is one depressing prayer! I remember as a child wondering if death was a common side effect of bedtime. It made me not want to fall asleep, lest I "die before I wake!" My mom and I laugh about it now, but at the time it surely made an impact! As I got older, I graduated from the "save my soul prayers" to "wish-list prayers." Each night I went over my inventory of wants with God just to make sure we were on the same page. It went something like this:

Dear God, Please, please, please help me make an A on my history test even though I didn't really study. And please let Mark like me and not Missy. And please make my brother vaporize into thin air. Amen.

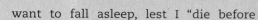

As I graduated on to middle school, they took on a more urgent tone. The requests centered on making cheerleader, winning track meets, getting invited to the cool parties, and praying my parents wouldn't find out I got called into the office for passing notes in class.

By high school I had pretty much decided that God had his favorites and I was not one of them. I assumed that because he didn't always answer my prayers in the way I wanted, he either (a) must not be listening, or (b) must not care. Either way I didn't see the purpose in prayer, so my prayers died down to the occasional "flair prayers." If I was in some sort of crisis, I might toss up a flair prayer to God to see if it yielded results.

When I finally became a Christian late in my college years, it quickly became clear that I had a lot to learn about prayer. It was then that I learned the ACTS model of prayer that I still use today. I have taught my children this model, as well. ACTS is an acrostic that stands for adoration (or praise), confession, thanks, and supplication (making requests of God for others or ourselves).

THE ACTS MODEL

WHEN YOU PRAY, START BY THINKING OF HIS DIVINE CHARACTERISTICS AND "ADORING" HIM WITH PRAISES OF THOSE CHARACTERISTICS.

Adoration

The "A" of ACTS stands for adoration. It seems only fitting that prayer to a Holy God should begin with acknowledgment to his divine characteristics and attributes. When you pray, start by thinking of his divine characteristics and adoring him with praises of those characteristics. Examples would be his holiness, ability and willingness to forgive, patience with us when we go astray, ability to love us perfectly and completely, his provision of his Son, his role as Creator, etc. It is an expression of faith when we take the focus off our own needs and direct our attention to the very one who promises to meet our needs.

Confession

The "C" of ACTS stands for confession. Confession is basically agreeing with God over our sin and feeling sorrow for our sin. Unless we think and feel the same way about our sin that God does, we will not repent of our sin (turn from our sin and turn back to God) (see 2 Corinthians 7:10). When I get to the confession part of my prayer time, I try to think of specific ways that I have sinned that day rather than make a general sweeping statement. An example would be: "Lord, I confess that I was wrong when I gossiped on the phone today and said that so-and-so was having marital problems." This is better than a general "Lord, I confess that sometimes I slip and

*U*NLESS WE THINK AND FEEL THE SAME WAY ABOUT OUR SIN THAT GOD DOES, WE WILL NOT REPENT OF OUR SIN.

gossip." If my confession involves a wrongdoing against another person, many times I am convicted in my prayer time to make it right with the person and ask his or her forgiveness. When you develop the habit of confessing your sins on a daily basis and

acknowledge God's forgiveness, it reminds you that sin is a serious matter in the eyes of God. However, remember that no sin is too big for the forgiveness of God. First John 1:9 promises that "If we confess our sins, [God] is faithful and righteous to forgive us our sins and to cleanse us from all unrighteousness."

Thanks

The "T" in ACTS stands for thanks. When I think of the need to thank God, I am reminded of the ten lepers spoken of in Luke 17:12–18. They all cried out to Jesus to have pity on them and heal them. He responded to their cries and told them to "Go and show yourselves to the priests," and then he healed them on their way. Unfortunately, only one bothered to return and thank him. Jesus asked the man, "Were not 10 cleansed? Where are the nine? Didn't any return to give glory to God except this foreigner?" Often, I am guilty, like the nine lepers, of failing to thank God for answered prayers.

One practical solution to this problem is to use a prayer journal. This can be done by using a blank notebook and dividing the pages into two columns. In one column, list your prayer requests, and n the other column, mark when and how the prayer was answered. When keeping a prayer journal, we are more likely to notice when God answers our prayers and offer him the thanks he deserves.

As hard as it is to remember to thank God when he answers your prayers, it is even harder to thank him when he answers your prayers but not in a

God is the father of compassion and the God of all comfort who is capable of comforting you in all your troubles (see 2 Cor. 1:3–4). Girls who learn to run to Jesus in times of sadness or suffering are less likely to turn to other unhealthy things (food, alcohol, drugs, shopping, busyness, sex outside of marriage, etc.) when seeking comfort. Only God can truly mend a broken heart.

It is important that you converse with God on a daily basis. Get in the habit of talking to him throughout your day as things come up. Run things past him. And sometimes sit in silence before him and listen for his still quiet voice. He waits for you each day and can't wait to talk to you.

Rejoice always! Pray constantly. Give thanks in everything, for this is God's will for you in Christ Jesus.
(1 Thessalonians 5:16–18)

way you had hoped. Nonetheless, in 1 Thessalonians 5:18, God calls us to "give thanks in everything." In addition to thanking God for answered prayers, we should also express thanks for things that we might otherwise take for granted. This includes the blessings of family, extended family, church family, a place to live, food to eat, freedom to worship, and on and on. Regardless of your circumstances, you should never run out of things for which to thank God.

GOD IS THE FATHER OF COMPASSION AND THE GOD OF ALL COMFORT WHO IS CAPABLE OF COMFORTING YOU IN ALL YOUR TROUBLES.

Supplication

SThe "S" in ACTS stands for supplication. Supplication is when we submit our requests to God on behalf of ourselves and others. As a habit of thinking of others first, try to lift up your own needs last. Be honest and transparent before God. Are you hurting? Tell him. Are you scared? Tell him. Talk to him as you would your very best friend and trust that your prayers are heard.

your instruction manual for living

Are you the type to read the instruction manual when you get something new? Do people like that really exist? I know they do because I married one of them. When my husband and I were engaged, we had quite a few wedding showers and received many appliances. After one particular shower, he stopped by my apartment to see the loot. But what he did next, I will never forget. He then proceeded to gather up all the instruction manuals out of the appliance boxes, and he began to read them. But it gets worse. As he read through them one by one, he would mark them up with a highlighter pen! You would have thought the guy was studying for a test or something! When he finished, he handed me the stack and said, "Here, I made it real easy for you. Just read the highlighted portions, and that should be enough." It was at that

> All Scripture is insired by God and is profitable for teaching, for rebuking, for correcting, for training in righteousness, so that the man of God may be complete, equipped for every good work.
> (2 Timothy 3:16–17)

moment that I knew we were total opposites. I don't think I had ever even saved an instruction manual, much less read one, in my entire life. I mean, if the thing couldn't be figured out by just turning it on, it wasn't worth having. Of course, we have since learned to compromise and meet in the middle. He does his part by highlighting the instruction manuals, and I do my part by promising not to throw them away. Even though I poke fun at his habit of highlighting instruction manuals, I must admit that it has saved us time and money down the road as he knows in advance how best to care for each appliance and where to look if it begins to have problems.

Sometimes I hear people joke and say they wish life had come with some sort of instruction manual. The good news is that it does! God has left us the Bible as our instruction manual. How sad it is that most

everyone in this country owns a Bible but few will recognize its power. It contains everything we need to know to make it through life. Critics will argue that it is just a book. The real proof is in the number of changed lives of those who have come to depend on it as the inspired Word of God.

"All Scripture is insired by God and is profitable for teaching, for rebuking, for correcting, for training in righteousness, so that the man of God may be complete, equipped for every good work" (2 Timothy 3:16–17).

One thing that catches many Christian youth off guard when they go to college is the number of vocal critics they encounter who deny the authenticity of the Bible as the inspired Word of God. Many of these critics are college professors! The sad thing is that most Christian youth do not have a ready defense for the critics. They have never been taught the facts regarding the accuracy of the Bible.

Can the Bible be trusted as the accurate source of God's truth? You bet! Christians do not need to check their brains at the door when it comes to supporting the validity of the Bible. When the critics speak out against the accuracy of the Bible, will you have a ready defense? So, what are the factors that lend to the Bible's credibility as our instruction manual for living?

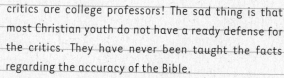

ARCHEOLOGY: An overwhelming amount of archaeological evidence supports the validity of the Bible. For example, a recent study of ancient Jericho concluded that the walls did tumble down as the Bible indicates. More than twenty-five thousand archeological sites have been discovered which connect to the Old Testament period. These discoveries have provided much evidence to support hundreds of scriptural assertions. In fact, not a single archaeological discovery has contradicted or disproved a biblical assertion.

CONSISTENCY OF SCRIPTURE OVER THE YEARS: When I participate in friendly debates concerning Christianity, one of the most common arguments I hear against the Bible is that it could not possibly reflect the original documents since it has been translated so many

Not a single archaeological discovery has contradicted or disproved a biblical assertion.

times over the years. One Bible scholar concluded from a lifetime of studying early documentary evidence, that "not more than one-thousandth part of the New Testament is affected by differences of reading." He added that there were only insignificant variations in grammar or spelling between various documents.[1]

When it comes to the dependability of the Old Testament, 1947 marked one of the greatest

archaeological finds of all time with the discovery of the famed Dead Sea Scrolls. The scrolls were contained in ancient jars found in caves in the valley of the Dead Sea. They date back to 150 BC to AD 70. In this significant find, the entire Book of Isaiah was found, as well as fragments of every Book of the Old Testament except Esther. When the scrolls were compared to the Masoretic text written some thousand years later by Jewish scribes (from which our Old Testament of today is derived), it resulted in remarkable accuracy. This is not surprising given the fact that great care was taken by scribes in copying the original text. Because they thought they were documenting the Word of God, and they were devoted to accuracy. They were known to wipe the pen clean before writing the name of God, copy one letter at a time, and count the letters of the original and the one copied to confirm accurate transmission. In most cases, if an error was found, the entire copy was destroyed.

FULFILLED PROPHECY: Dr. Hugh Ross, a well known astrophysicist, says that out of twenty five hundred predictions contained in the Bible regarding the future, some two thousand have alread

and highlighting key points as you go. Your life is more likely to function properly should you actually read the instructions. It's the only instruction manual I've read and without it, I'd be lost. ✱

1. Scholar: F. J. A. Hort quoted in *Know Why You Believe* 4th edition by Paul E. Little (Downer's Grove, Ill.: InterVarsity Press), 77.
2. Ibid.

been fulfilled. Every one of these predictions have been fulfilled in detail without a single error. Dr. Ross has calculated that the probability of two thousand predictions coming true without error is 1 in 10 to the 2000th power.[2] Science considers any probability greater than 1 in 10 to the 50th power as impossible. So how was it possible? There is only one explanation: God, who knows the future, inspired the writers of these predictions to write them down in text that today constitutes the Bible.

So you see, you can't ask for a better or more dependable instruction manual than that. You'd be better off to follow my husband's example of reading the instruction manual

the
secret
to a
happy life

What if I told you there was proof that if you read a particular book on a regular basis it would lead to a more positive outlook on life? Would you read it? Chances are good you have at least one in your home, considering it's the best-selling book of all time. Hopefully, your Bible is sitting on your nightstand rather than gathering dust on a bookshelf. If not, it's time to dust the Good Book off and dive in—your happiness awaits!

Here are the facts:

> Eighty-two percent of regular Bible readers described themselves as "at peace," versus 58 percent of those who said they never read the Bible.

> Seventy-eight percent of regular Bible readers said they felt "happy" all or most of the time, versus 67 percent of nonreaders.

> Sixty-eight percent of regular Bible readers said they were "full of joy," versus 44 percent who said they never read the Bible.

> Eighty-one percent of regular Bible readers said they were satisfied with life in general, versus 63 percent of those who don't read the Bible.

> Ninety-four percent of regular Bible readers believe that life has a clear purpose and meaning, versus 76 percent of nonreaders.

Source: "Study: Bible Gives Readers More Positive Outlook on Life," *Austin American Statesman* (13 November 2001); study originally conducted by Barna Research Group and published in *Newsweek*.

a soldier's call to duty

I'm part of the fellowship of the unashamed. I have Holy Spirit power. The die has been cast. I have stepped over the line. The decision has been made. I'm a disciple of His. I won't look back, let up, slow down, back away, or be still.

My past has been redeemed, my present makes sense, and my future is secure. I am finished and done with low living, sight walking, small planning, smooth knees, colorless dreams, tamed visions, mundane talking, cheap living, and dwarfed goals.

I no longer need preeminence, prosperity, position, promotions, plaudits, or popularity. I don't have to be right, first, tops, recognized, praised, regarded, or rewarded. I now live by faith, lean on His presence, walk by patience, lift by prayer, and labor by power.

My face is set, my gait is fast, my goal is heaven, my road is narrow, my way rough, my companions few, my guide reliable, my mission clear. I cannot be bought, compromised, detoured, lured away, turned back, deluded, or delayed. I will not flinch in the face of sacrifice, hesitate in the presence of the adversary, negotiate at the table of the enemy, ponder in the pool of popularity, or meander in the maze of mediocrity.

I won't give up, shut up, or let up, until I have stayed up, stored up, prayed up, paid up, and preached up for the cause of Christ. I am a disciple of Jesus. I must go till He comes, give till I drop, preach till all know, and work until He stops me. And when He comes for His own, He will have no problem recognizing me—my banner will be clear.

—Anonymous

Share in suffering as a good soldier of Christ Jesus. (2 Timothy 2:3)

why are we here in this

do you not know that the runners in a stadium all race, but only one receives the prize? Run in such a way that you may win. Now everyone who competes exercises self-control in everything. However, they do it to receive a perishable crown, but we an imperishable one. (1 Corinthians 9:24—25)

I wonder how many Christians wear themselves out running for the world's prizes. Prizes that will turn to dust someday. I've heard it said that you never see a U-haul behind a hearse. Why gather prizes that we can't take with us when we can invest our time and energy into things with eternal value. So what does it look like to run for a crown that will last forever? The next verse in the passage above answers the question: "Therefore I do not run like one who runs aimlessly" (1 Corinthians 9:26a). Another translation says it this way: "So I run straight to the goal with purpose in every step" (NLT). If we are to run with purpose in our steps, we must first be clear on what our purpose is in life. If someone had asked me what my purpose in life was at your age, I would not have had a clue.

For Christians our purpose in life is clear: To know God and make him known. It's that simple. So, what exactly does it look like? Let's break it down.

KNOW GOD

Our chief goal is to know God. When we are young, we tend to think that life is all about us. Some people

> God put us on this earth to get to know and worship him.

never mature past the "me-first" mind-set and will go to their graves having served only themselves. God put us on this earth to get to know and worship him. He has provided the Bible

as a means to know him. It is a revelation of his character and a constant reminder of his love and mercy. If you do not regularly spend time reading your Bible, it will be hard to get to know him. If your schedule is overloaded with homework and activities, there are devotionals available that focus on short passages of Scripture. If you are not using a devotional book, I recommend reading through the New Testament if you have never done so before. Keep in mind that the first four books of the New Testament (Matthew, Mark, Luke, and John) are called the "four gospels" and give an account of Jesus birth, life, death, and resurrection from four different authors. Also pay close attention to the book of Romans. It contains many lifelong principles that, if learned early, can build your trust in God and prepare you for the future. Get in the habit of highlighting or underlining verses that have

great big world?

special meaning to you. Sometimes, I write meaningful verses down on note cards for the purpose of memorizing them later. Most importantly, when you are reading, try to get in the habit of asking yourself, How does this passage apply to my life today?

Another way to "know God," is to communicate with him on a regular basis through prayer. Prayer doesn't

MAKE HIM KNOWN
SAVE THE BABY WHALES
STOP GLOBAL WARMING
HAVE YOU HUGGED A TREE TODAY?
VISUALIZE WORLD PEACE

Bumper stickers crack me up. Sometimes I wonder, with all the worthy causes out there, how people can rationalize putting their energy into

some of the crusades they choose. With challenges like finding a cure for AIDS, feeding the hungry, clothing the poor, and how about, the most important one: saving the lost, it seems ridiculous to funnel time, money, and energy into things that don't matter for eternity. I remember years back when the development of a new mall in Austin was halted because some environmental extremist group claimed that an endangered cave beetle might be hiding under rocks where the proposed mall was to be built. If these rare beetles were in fact there, they claimed the development would kill them off once and for all. The beetle was less than an eighth of an inch in length, had no eyes, and lived in total darkness under rocks. I had to drive ten extra miles to another mall so a cave beetle, that no one had actually even seen, could camp out under a rock in total darkness. Sounds like the kind of bug that could easily survive

We have been given the cause of spreading the gospel message of Christ. That is our number one job duty.

have to be saved for bedtime and emergencies. Get in the habit of running things past God throughout your day. The more you communicate with him, the better you will know him. Think about it, if you have a best friend but you never call her or talk to her at school, how can you really know her? The same is true when it comes to our relationship with God.

under a mall concrete slab, if you ask me. Anyway, the mall finally got built, but in order to make the beetle-maniacs happy, the developers had to set up a place in the mall devoted to educate the public about the cave beetle. I wish I could give you more details, but like most everyone else in Austin, I've never dropped by to see it.

passed away, and look, new things have come. Now everything is from God, who reconciled us to Himself through Christ and gave us the ministry of reconciliation: that is, in Christ, God was reconciling the world to Himself, not counting their trespasses against them, and He has committed the message of reconciliation to us. Therefore, we are ambassadors for Christ; certain

reconciliation. Don't let the big words throw you off—it simply means that he has entrusted us with the good news message that Christ paid the price for our sins and is counting on us to deliver the good news to others.

Our jobs begin today. There is much work to do in the harvest, and every ambassador is needed. Your mission field is your school,

He has entrusted us with the good news message that Christ paid the price for our sins and is counting on us to deliver the good news to others.

Christians have been given a cause far more important than saving the environment, the baby whales, the rain forests, and yes, even the cave beetles. We have been given the cause of spreading the gospel message of Christ. That is our number one job duty. See if you can find our job title in the passage below:

Therefore if anyone is in Christ, there is a new creation; old things have

that God is appealing through us, we plead on Chist's behalf, "Be reconciled to God" (2 Corithians 5:17–20).

We are his ambassadors! An ambassador is an "official messenger and representative." That is an overwhelming thought when you consider that we work directly for God. It is our job to make him look good. The passage above spells out our job duty: He has committed to us the message of

neighborhood, job, and yes, even your church. As long as there is just one person who has yet to hear, we have a job to do. Your purpose in life is to know God and make him known. Anything else is running aimlessly. ✳

Get Real!

Everyone hates a fake—so start getting honest with yourself and God! Take this quiz and find out if the real you needs a spiritual makeover.

1. It's the end of the day, and you haven't made time for God; so you:

a) say a quick good-night prayer and hit the sheets.

b) make some quality time with God before you snooze.

c) don't really think about it and IM your friends before catching some z's.

2. Your government teacher openly ridicules Christians; you:

a) stay silent, hoping he won't remember you are a Christian.

b) aren't afraid to stand up for what is right, even though your grades might take a beating.

c) join in, even though that's not how you really feel inside.

3. Your best friend wants you to skip last period with her and go to the lake; you:

a) tell her you aren't feeling good but would go if you felt better.

b) decline and let her know dishonesty is a sin in your book but will go to the lake another time when you don't have to skip school.

c) give her the keys to your car and tell her to meet you in five minutes (you have to change into your swimsuit first).

4. It's Friday night and several close friends are going downtown with fake IDs to try to get into a popular college club; you:

a) pretend you're grounded and tell them to be careful.

b) remind them that you can't hang out with them if they're going to do illegal things and invite them to hang out with you instead.

c) borrow your sister's old ID and tell your mom you're going to a girls' sleepover.

5. You're sitting at youth group and the most unpopular girl sits down in the chair next to you; you:

a) don't want to move but convince your friends to come sit with you so you don't have to sit next to her by yourself.

b) ask her how her week was, try to get to know her a little better, and invite her to dinner after youth group.

c) pretend you have a phone call, and go to the back to see where the cute guys are sitting.

6. It's Monday morning, first period, and you forgot to do your math homework because you went out of town with your family; you:

a) embellish the truth and tell your teacher you had a family emergency and ask for an extension.

b) tell your teacher you completely forgot and ask if she can let you turn it in tomorrow morning.

c) borrow your friend's homework and copy it quickly before class.

7. You're at a friend's birthday party and they start playing spin the bottle; you:

a) tell them you won't play but will spin the bottle for everyone else.

b) let them know that casually kissing all your guy friends is not something you feel honors them or you and politely let them know you would rather head home.

c) are glad someone finally thought of a way to liven this dead party!

If you answered mostly (a): Get a backbone—you know what's right but sometimes have a hard time standing up for what you believe. Find a Christian friend that can keep you accountable as well as encourage you to stand up for God. Get your approval from God and not your friends, and he will give you the courage to do what's right, even when everyone around you is making wrong choices.

If you answered mostly (b): You get it—congratulations, you balance real life with godly values, and you're not afraid to stand up for what you believe. Everyone who knows you knows you're not ashamed to be a Christian, and you stick to your Christian standards. Stay strong and continue to make God first in your life.

If you answered mostly (c): Get a spiritual makeover—you crave the approval of your friends, which often leads to wrong choices or situations that leave you unsatisfied. Sin can be fun for a season, but eventually the separation from God leaves us feeling empty and alone. It's never too late to ask God to be the center of your life. Spend time with him daily, and he will change your heart and desires. Eventually it won't matter what others are doing; you will realize you have a deeper peace when you obey God instead.

Material provided by Julie Shannan.

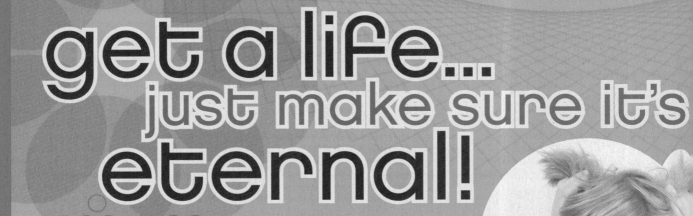

get a life...
just make sure it's
eternal!

When I was your age, I was not a Christian. However, I vividly remember friends asking me every so often, "Are you a Christian?" I recall feeling somewhat uncomfortable with the question and not quite sure how to answer. I was too embarrassed to confess that I didn't really know what was involved in "being a Christian." So I always told them yes. Most didn't persist any further, and I breathed a sigh of relief. When I finally did become a Christian in my college years, the gospel made sense and became clear to me for the first time. If you are not sure where you stand regarding Christianity, I encourage you to read carefully over the basics of Christianity below and what it means to be a Christian. If at the end you realize you have never responded to God's offer of forgiveness, would you consider doing so? God is chasing after you and actively drawing you to himself. You will never face a more important decision in the course of your life than the decision to accept or reject Jesus Christ as your personal Savior. I pray you will accept him.

HOW TO BECOME A CHRISTIAN

The central theme of the Bible is God's love for you and for all people. This love was revealed when Jesus Christ, the Son of God, came into the world as a human being, lived a sinless life, died on the cross, and rose from the dead. Because Christ died, your sins can be forgiven, and because he conquered death, you can have eternal life. You can know for sure what will become of you after you die.

You have probably heard the story of God's love referred to as the gospel. The word *gospel* simply means "good news." The gospel is the good news that, because of what Christ has done, we can be forgiven and can live forever.

But this gift of forgiveness and eternal life cannot be yours unless you willingly accept it. God requires an individual response from you. The following verses from the Bible show God's part and your part in this process:

GOD'S LOVE IS REVEALED IN THE BIBLE

"For God loved the world in this way: He gave His One and Only Son, so that everyone who believes in Him will not perish but have eternal life." (John 3:16)

God loves you. He wants to bless your life and make it full and complete. And he wants to give you a life which will last forever, even after you experience physical death.

WE ARE SINFUL

"For all have sinned and fall short of the glory of God." (Romans 3:23)

You may have heard someone say, "I'm only human—nobody's perfect." This verse says the same thing: We are all sinners. We all do things that we know are wrong. And that's why we feel estranged from God—because God is holy and good, and we are not.

SIN HAS A PENALTY

"For the wages of sin is death." (Romans 6:23a)

Just as criminals must pay the penalty for their crimes, sinners must pay the penalty for their sins. If you continue to sin, you will pay the penalty of spiritual death: You will not only die physically; you will also be separated from our holy God for all eternity. The Bible teaches that those who choose to remain separated from God will spend eternity in a place called hell.

CHRIST HAS PAID OUR PENALTY!

"But God proves His own love for us in that while we were still sinners Christ died for us!" (Romans 5:8)

The Bible teaches that Jesus Christ, the sinless Son of God, has paid the penalty for all your sins. You may think you have to lead a good life and do good deeds before God will love you. But the Bible says that Christ loved you enough to die for you, even when you were rebelling against him.

SALVATION IS A FREE GIFT

"For by grace you are saved through faith, and this not from yourselves; it is God's gift—not from works, so that no one can boast." (Ephesians 2:8–9)

The word *grace* means "undeserved favor." It means God is offering you something you could never provide for yourself: forgiveness of sins and eternal life. God's gift to you is free. You do not have to work for a gift. All you have to do is joyfully receive it, Believe with all your heart that Jesus Christ died for you!

CHRIST IS AT YOUR HEART'S DOOR

"Listen! I stand at the door and knock. If anyone hears My voice and opens the door, I will come in to him and have dinner with him, and he with Me." (Revelation 3:20)

Jesus Christ wants to have a personal relationship with you. Picture, if you will, Jesus Christ standing at the door of your heart (the door of your emotions, intellect, and will). Invite him in; he is waiting for you to receive him into your heart and life.

YOU MUST RECEIVE HIM

"But to all who did receive Him, He gave them the right to be children of God, to those who believe in His name." (John 1:12)

When you receive Christ into your heart, you become a child of God and have the privilege of talking to him in prayer at any time about anything. The Christian life is a personal relationship to God through Jesus Christ. And best of all, it is a relationship that will last for all eternity.

Therefore, if anyone is in Christ, there is a new creation; old thing have passed away, and look, new things have come. (2 Corinthians 5:17)

Source: Taken from "Your Christian Life" 1965, 1968, as "Aids to Christian Living," 1986 as "Practical Steps in Christian Living," 1995 as "Beginning Your Christian Life," 1997 as "Your Christian Life," Billy Graham Evangelistic Association.